Praise for Alicia Partnoy's ٦
Tales of Disappearance & Su

"Lyrical, ebullient, charming, vigorous and ingenious..."
— *San Francisco Chronicle*

"Alicia Partnoy's accounts are courageous, understated, chilling; and they are very well written."
— Bobbie Ann Mason

"Remarkable... for her flinty humor and her determination to take joy from any source—the smell of rain, the imagined taste of a soft drink, the sight of her own feet through a loosely tied blindfold."
—Tobias Wolff

"Strength and courage...is well portrayed..."
—*The Nation*

"A testimony to the healing powers of art and imagination, of humor and compassion..."
—*The Guardian*

"The common thread of Partnoy's tales is a message of love for humanity..."
— *Cleveland Plain Dealer*

"Partnoy's triumph is to have discovered under her blindfold another pair of eyes, eyes that found a reason to survive in a world that did not deserve her. It is our privilege to look through those eyes for a short time, and to be reminded that we who claim freedom as our birthright must raise our voices, again and again, on behalf of those imprisoned in all the Little Schools around the world."
— *Pittsburgh Post-Gazette*

"Partnoy's spirit of resistance is also a spirit of creativity and hope ."
– *In These Times*

"*The Little School* is compelling precisely because torture, political repression, and inhumanity are brought home to us in vivid, felt particulars that shatter our indifference...The most overwhelming lesson of *The Little School* is that the poetry of seeing can sustain us."

— *Belles Lettres*

"*The Little School* is more than a written witness to social injustice: it is a work of art... Partnoy shares the most intimate moments of her life with great dignity. "

— *Hurricane Alice*

"*The Little School* is a collection of short stories, as delicate as cobwebs...As if issued from a spiritually quiet, often humorous, center of a violent storm, the stories depict the moments of gentle absurdity in prison life "

— *Women's Review of Books*

"What makes Partnoy's voice so powerful is that it conveys a strength and clarity of vision that makes us aware of the incredible resilience and enormous possibilities of the human spirit "

Sojourner

"Alicia Partnoy has kept the precious and courageous voices of this drama from slipping inevitably into an oblivion that they do not deserve..."

— *Washington Review*

You Can't Drown the Fire:

Latin American Women Writing in Exile

Edited by

Alicia Partnoy

Cleis Press
Pittsburgh • San Francisco

Every possible effort has been made to ensure that permission has been granted for use of the material printed herein. Any errors to this effect will be duly noted and corrected in future editions: *Domitila Barrios de Chungara*: from *Aquí también Domitila*, reprinted by permission of Siglo XXI Editores, Mexico. Copyright 1985 by David Acebey; *Olga Behar*: from *Las guerras de la paz*, Planeta, Bogota, reprinted by permission of the author. Copyright 1985 by Olga Behar; *Alicia Dujovne Ortiz*: from *Vamos a Vladivostok!*, reprinted by permission of the author. Copyright 1987 by Alicia Dujovne Ortiz. *Julia Esquivel*: from *Threatened with Resurrection: Amenazado de Resurrección*, reprinted by permission of Brethren. Copyright 1982 by Julia Esquivel; *Alaíde Foppa*: "Woman" from *Women Brave in the Face of Danger*, ed. Margaret Randall, The Crossing Press, Trumansburg, NY, reprinted by permission of Margaret Randall. Copyright 1985 by Margaret Randall; "Words" from *Las palabras y el tiempo (Words & Time)*, La Vida Press, Flushing, NY, reprinted by permission of the translators, Rozenn Frère and Dennis Nurkse; *Griselda Gambaro*: from *Dios no nos quiere contentos*, Lumen, Barcelona, reprinted by permission of the author. Copyright 1979 by Griselda Gambaro. *Isabel Letelier*: from *First Harvest: The Institute for Policy Studies, 1963-1983*, reprinted by permission of IPS, Washington D.C. Copyright 1980 by Isabel Letelier; *Rigoberta Menchú*: from *Le Monde*, Spanish edition (Mexico), December 1986, reprinted by permission of the interviewer, César Chelala; *Ana Guadalupe Martínez*: from *Las cárceles clandestinas de El Salvador*; *Pastora*: from *Nuevo Diario*, Nicaragua, September 2, 1984; *Cristina Peri Rossi*: from *La tarde del dinosaurio*, Plaza y Janes, Barcelona; reprinted by permission of the author. Copyright 1985 by Cristina Peri Rossi; *Clara Nieto Ponce de León*: from *NACLA Report*, Vol. XXI, No. 4, July/August 1987, reprinted by permission of the author. Copyright 1987 by Clara Nieto de Ponce de León; *Laura Restrepo*: from *Historia de una traición*, Plaza y Janes, Bogota, reprinted by permission of the author. Copyright 1986 by Laura Restrepo; *Mercedes Sosa*: from *Argentina: Como matar la cultura*, edited by AIDA, Editorial Revolucion, Spain, 1981, reprinted by permission of the publisher; *María Gravina Telechea*: from *Lázaro vuela rojo*, Casa de las Americas, Havana, reprinted by permission of the author; *Marta Traba*: from *En cualquier lugar*, reprinted by permission of Siglo XXI Editores, Bogota. Copyright 1984 by Marta Traba; *María Tila Uribe*: from *Desde Adentro*, reprinted by permission of the author. Copyright 1984 by María Tila Uribe; *Luisa Valenzuela*: from *Strange Things Happen Here: Twenty-six Short Stories and a Novel*, Harcourt Brace Jovanovich, New York; reprinted by permission of the author. Copyright 1979 by Luisa Valenzuela; *Cecilia Vicuña*: from the *American Poetry Review*, March/April 1987; and from *La Wikuña* (unpublished), reprinted by permission of the author. Copyright 1987 by Cecilia Vicuña.

Published in the United States by Cleis Press, P.O. Box 8933, Pittsburgh, Pennsylvania 15221, and P.O. Box 14684, San Francisco, California 94114.
Printed in the United States.
First Edition.
10 9 8 7 6 5 4 3 2
Cover design: Peter Ivey
Typeset: Will Miner & his Wild Bats
ISBN: 0-939416-16-6 cloth
ISBN: 0-939416-17-4 paper
Library of Congress Catalog Card Number: 88-70218

You Can't Drown the Fire

With special thanks to

Translators:

Regina M. Kreger
Natalia López
Elinor Randall
Andrea Vincent
Emma Buenaventura
Marcela Kogan
Zoë Anglessey
María Negroni
Charlie Roberts
Vladimir Klimenko
Sally Hanlon
Nena Terrell
Dennis Nurkse
Rozenn Frère
Helen Lane
María Elena Acevedo
René Calderón
María Elena Caracheo
Sister Caridad Inda
Philip Wheaton
Eliot Weinberger
Judith Weiss
Magda Bogin
Sophie Black
Margaret Randall

Interviewers:

César Chelala
Noema Viezzer
Adriana Angel
Julio Cardenal

Editor:

Felice Newman

Editorial Support·

Laura Lynn Brown

In memory of those
who were exiled from life
So they rest in peace
their bones nurturing
    their motherland,
their souls nurturing
our fight

Contents

III. THE TORCH THAT SHEDS MY LIGHT: ESSAY

IV. SPARKS OF FURY AND SHOOTING STARS: POETRY

V. SETTING DISTANCE ON FIRE: LETTERS

SELECTED BIBLIOGRAPHY

Introduction

T he women whose fires will speak to you from these pages have suffered all forms of persecution. From the Salvadoran girl who witnessed the assassination of her family to the Argentine mother of a disappeared; from the Colombian journalist whose name was found on a death squad hit list to the Uruguayan writer expelled by the military; from the Guatemalan catechist who lost three brothers to repression to the Chilean activist, jailed and tortured—each of these women was forced into exile. Each left her homeland as a painful, but unavoidable, alternative to the loss of her life, her spirit, her creativity.

It is only in the past decade that a few of these voices have begun to be heard. The testimonies of Rigoberta Menchú and Domitila Barrios were only recently printed and widely circulated. The talents of Marta Traba and Luisa Valenzuela—like Isabel Allende—have finally been recognized and internationally praised. And while some doors have opened for Claribel Alegría, who has traveled this country with her poems, her testimonies, her essays and her incredible patience, the works of Alaíde Foppa are practically unknown. Cristina Peri Rossi, Griselda Gambaro, Alicia Dujovne Ortiz are names that, in the United States, only the initiate might have heard. Yet, these women were published, well-known writers before being forced into exile.

11

After publication of my book about life in an Argentine concentration camp, I sensed a yearning in the United States for writings by other Latin American women, who had also been victims of repression. University professors and students, people in the peace movement and in Amnesty International, feminists and others concerned for Latin America voiced a genuine interest. With the belief that these writings could become a tool for education rather than mere fashion, the women who published my first book quickly responded to my observations and needs. I felt the urgency of bringing the voices of my sisters into this language that I had learned with such difficulty. I strongly needed to share with those sisters the readers who had responded with solidarity to my tales of *The Little School*. The women of Cleis Press offered to publish this anthology.

I began the search for manuscripts with three goals in mind: to build cultural bridges, to destroy stereotypes about Latin American women, and to denounce political repression in our countries.

The building of bridges would have been impossible without translators who contributed the strong, reliable material of their expertise, their love of language, their commitment to Latin America.

Stereotypes about Latin American women mushroom out of the refusal to perceive the diversity of our lives. During my years of exile in the United States, I have met many people who jump to hasty, and erroneous, conclusions about us. For some, we victims of repression are peasant women who suffered persecution only because of the political involvement of our husbands and brothers; for others, we are all urban intellectuals who became too outspoken to be tolerated by our repressive governments.

The voices of Central and South American women, who share a language and a history, will themselves destroy these stereotypes. Grassroots organizers, trade unionists, representatives of student organizations, investigative reporters, outspoken leaders of professional associations, writers, human rights activists — Latin American women have claimed recognition as participants in the political lives of our countries. However, we still encounter discrimination: for those of us who have risked our lives for political and social change, there is seldom a position of power available in government. Yet, there is one realm in which we have not faced discrimination: Repression.

Yes, these voices speak in the rhythms of a Latin America struggling for freedom and justice. They are, however, as different as the histories of their individual countries; their approach to language varies as do their ages, their goals, their tastes, and the quality of formal education available to them. Their political perspectives are also as diverse. Yet, all of these women share one lucky condition: none was born under the sign of passivity.

In gathering these voices, I asked for writings in Spanish by women from Central and South America who had left their countries after 1970. The seventies had witnessed an increase of state terrorism in Latin America. Desperate oligarchies and multinational corporations resorted to their local military to curtail the social transformations that jeopardized their interests. The doctrine of national security, an ideology embraced by many South American armies, provided the justification to annihilate large numbers of people. These armies saw their nations threatened by an internal enemy. Soon, that enemy was the entire population. Military leaders, trained at the School of the Americas at the Panama Canal, feared they would lose control to civilian governments that would shun U.S. intervention. The military coups in Chile (1973), Uruguay (1973), Argentina (1976), resulted in the spreading of the doctrine of national security. Political prisoners, arrested in any of those countries, were transferred without respect for borders or international treaties, killed or disappeared in a Hell without frontiers.

By the late seventies, the number of 'disappeared' had dramatically increased to 90,000. Those who disappeared were kidnapped by the authorities, kept in unknown locations, tortured and eventually killed in secrecy. Argentine torturers were quick to aid Guatemalan repression, the Bolivian coup of 1980, and the training of the 'contras' who sow terror in Central America. Entire towns were bombed in El Salvador, forcing large masses of people into exile. Hundreds of thousands are still seeking refuge in the United States, a country that provides the means to repress them. Today, thousands of Colombians are fleeing their country where a multitude of right-wing death squads, condoned by the government, terrorizes political activists and journalists who do not endorse their ideas. In Chile, similar groups have recently threatened artists, journalists and university professors while the government of dictator Pinochet denies any connection. In the seventies, repressive governments perfected their criminal ways of dealing with popular unrest. Under military dictatorships or puppet 'democracies,' disappearance, torture, assassination, imprisonment or expulsion from the country became predictable hazards for any dissidents, their families — children included — and their support networks. Millions of Latin Americans left their countries.

The drawbacks of having established 1970 as a limit became evident when I received a letter from Carmen Batsche. Carmen, a Guatemalan, had fled to Argentina as a child with her exiled mother in 1954, after the coup that overthrew Jacobo Arbenz. Her testimony could not pass unheard. Nor could we deny voice to the experience of Paraguayans, who have lived under the same dictatorship since 1954. Only Dolly Filártiga, who had left Paraguay in 1977, sent her contribution. Central and South America proved to be too large a territory for my networking abilities. Some countries are under represented, others are absent.

The works in this anthology were written while in exile, with the exception of Olga Behar's report. The publication of *Las guerras de la paz* (excerpted here) unleashed a wave of death threats that forced her to leave Colombia.

In the process of contacting as many contributors as possible, I became really aware of the magnitude of the diaspora. Women called from my own neighborhood in Washington D.C., wrote from Spain and France, from California and Massachusetts, from Mexico and Uruguay, from every corner that could have been made into a new home. Women nurtured me with their observations: "Please accept a sister's suggestion: do not let this book become a whining sorrowful lamentation. We shouldn't let exile defeat us...," wrote Jacinta Escudos of El Salvador.

Initially, I defined exile as the forced departure from a person's homeland due to attacks or threats to her life, her family, or her work. This was challenged by the contributors. I soon realized that in countries where repression had taken the most arbitrary, disconcerting and destructive patterns, it was impossible to predict that a woman who had managed to leave before the personal attacks started would not have become a target had she chosen to stay. Internal exile was another issue raised by the women who corresponded with me. What about those who could never leave their country, but had to survive in silence and fear, banished in their own land? "Haven't Latin American women writers been in internal exile for centuries, their talents considered marginal?" asked poet Marjorie Agosín.

Writer and artist Cecilia Vicuña sent these enlightening words: "Chile is in exile from itself, the country has departed from itself. . . Internal and external exile are just the results of that general negation of our being, negation produced by the dictatorship and economic and cultural dependence." As much as I embrace her definition, I could not follow Cecilia's suggestion to include in this anthology "all women who, due to cultural, political and social reasons, cannot live in their countries or participate effectively in the lives of their homelands." That task, as well as the commitment of rescuing from oblivion the thousands of women who have died for peace and justice in Latin America, will demand our lifetime energies and those of future generations.

Many torches should be added to the thirty-five that burn so brightly in this anthology. That will be done tomorrow. For today, we must not miss the warmth, the energy, the arresting beauty of these fires. We must add our strength to the fires that comfort thousands at refugee camps, to these flames that burn injustice, these torches that cast our shadows on the walls of history.

Washington D.C.
February 1988

15

I.

They Won't Drown My Fire:
Testimony

Rigoberta Menchú
Guatemala

Rigoberta Menchú was born in Guatemala in 1962. A Quiché Indian, Rigoberta taught herself Spanish at the age of twenty. Among the founders of the Committee for the Peasants' Unity, she has traveled throughout the world as an ambassador of her suffering people. Her testimonial book, I, Rigoberta, *which she dictated to Elizabeth Burgos, was awarded the Casa de las Américas prize of Cuba.*

Things Have Happened to Me as in a Movie

I am Rigoberta Menchú; I am a native of the Quiché people of Guatemala. My life has been a long one. Things have happened to me as in a movie. My parents were killed in the repression. I have hardly any relatives living, or if I have, I don't know about them. It has been my lot to live what has been the lot of many, many Guatemalans.

We were a very poor family. All their lives my parents worked cutting cotton, cutting coffee. We lived about four months of the year on the high plain of Guatemala, where my father had a small piece of land; but that only supported us a short time, and then we had to go down to the plantations to get food.

During the whole time my mother was pregnant with me, she was on the plantation cutting coffee and cotton. I was paid twenty cents, many years ago, when I started to work in my town in Guatemala. There, the poor, the children, didn't have the opportunity for school; we did not have the opportunity to achieve any other life but working for food and to help our parents buy medicine for our little brothers and sisters. Two of my brothers died on the plantation cutting coffee. One of them got sick, couldn't be cured, and died. The other died when the landowner ordered the cotton sprayed while we were in the field. My brother was poisoned, there was no way to cure him and he died on the plantation, where we buried him.

We didn't know why those things happened. It's a miracle we were saved several times. When we got sick our mother looked for plants to cure us. The natives in Guatemala depended very much on nature. My mother cured us many times with the leaves of plants, with roots. That is how we managed to grow up. At ten years old, I started to work more in collaboration with my community, where my father, a local, native Mayan leader, was known by all the Indians of the region.

Little by little, my father got us involved in the concerns of the community. And so we grew up with that consciousness. My father was a catechist, and in Guatemala, a catechist is a leader of the community, and what he does especially is preach the Gospel. We, his children, began to evolve in the Catholic religion, and became catechists.

Little by little, we grew up — and really you can't say we started fighting only a short time ago, because it has been twenty-two years since my father fought over the land. The landowners wanted to take away our land, our little bit of land, and so my father fought for it. So he went to speak with the mayors, and with the judges in various parts of Guatemala. Afterwards, my father joined INTA, the land reform institution in Guatemala. For many years, my father was tricked because he did not speak Spanish. None of us spoke Spanish. So they made my father travel all over Guatemala to sign papers, letters, telegrams, which meant that not only he, but the whole community, had to sacrifice to pay the travel expenses. All this created an awareness in us from a very young age.

In the last years, my father was imprisoned many times, the first of those in 1954. My father landed in jail when he was accused of causing unrest among the population. When our father was in jail, the army kicked us out of our houses. They burned our clay pots. In our community we don't use iron or steel; we use clay pots, which we make ourselves with earth. But the army broke everything, and it was really hard for us to understand this situation.

Then my father was sentenced to eighteen years in prison, but he didn't serve them because we were able to work with lawyers to get him released. After a year and two months, my father got out of prison and returned home with more courage to go on fighting and much angrier because of what had happened. When that was over my mother had to go right to work as a maid in the city of Santa Cruz del Quiché, and all of us children had to go down to work on the plantations.

A short time later, my father was tortured by the landowners' bodyguards. Some armed men came to my house and took my father away. We got the community together and found my father lying in the road, far away, about two kilometers from home. My father was badly beaten and barely alive. The priests of the region had to come out to take my father to the hospital. He had been in the hospital for six months when we heard he was going to be taken out and killed. The landowners had been discussing it loudly, and the information came to us by way of their servants, who are also natives, and with whom we were very close. And so we had to find another place for my father, a private clinic the priests found for him so he would heal. But my father could no longer do hard work like he did before. A little later my father dedicated himself exclusively to working for the community, traveling, living off the land.

Several years passed, and again, in the year 1977, my father was sentenced to death. He landed in jail again. When we went to see him in the Pantán jail, the military told us they didn't want us to see my father, because he had committed many crimes. My mother went to Santa Cruz to find lawyers, and from them we learned that my father was going to be executed. When the time of the execution came, many union workers, students, peasants and some priests demonstrated for my father's freedom. My father was freed, but before he left he was threatened; he was told that he was going to be killed anyway for being a communist. From that moment on, my father had to carry out his activities in secret. He had to change the rhythm of his life. He lived hidden in several houses in Quiché, and then he went to the capital city. And so he became a leader of struggle for the peasants. It was then that my father said, "We must fight as Christians," and from there came the idea, along with other catechists, of forming Christian organizations which would participate in the process.

For us it was always a mystery how my father could carry out all those activities, which were very important, despite being illiterate. He never learned to read or write in his life. All his children were persecuted because of his activities, and our poverty really didn't help us defend ourselves, because we were in very sad circumstances.

All my father's activities had created a resentment in us because we couldn't have our parents' affection, because there were a lot of us children and a bigger worry was how to survive. On top of all this were the problems of the land, which upset my father very much. Many years before, rocks had fallen from the mountain and we had to go down from where we lived. When we went down and cultivated new land, the landowners appeared with documents and they told us the land was theirs before we came. But we knew very well the land had no owner before we got there.

They couldn't catch my father, but in the year 1979, they kidnapped one of my little brothers. He was sixteen. We didn't know who did it. We only knew that they were five armed men, with their faces covered. Since my father couldn't go out, we went with my mother and members of the community to make a complaint to the army, but they said they didn't know anything about what had happened to my brother. We went to City Hall, we went to all the jails in Guatemala, but we didn't find him. After many trips all over my mother was very upset. It had taken a lot for my brother to survive, and so for my mother it was very hard to accept his disappearance.

At that time the army published a bulletin saying there was going to be a guerrilla council. They said they had some guerrillas in their custody and that they were going to punish them in public. My mother said, "I hope to God my son shows up. I hope to God my son is there. I want to know what has happened to him." So we went to see what was happening. We walked for one day and almost the whole night to get to the other town. There were hundreds of soldiers who had almost the whole town surrounded, and who had gathered the people together to witness what they were going to do. There were natives of other areas as well as natives of that town. After a while an army truck arrived with twenty people who had been tortured in different ways. Among them we recognized my brother, who, along with the other prisoners, had been tortured for fifteen days. When my mother saw my little brother she almost gave herself away, but we had to calm her down, telling her that if she gave herself away she was going to die right there for being family of a guerrilla. We were crying, but almost all the rest of the people were crying also at the sight of the tortured people. They had pulled out my little brother's fingernails, they had cut off parts of his ears and other parts of his body, his lips, and he was covered with scars and swollen all over. Among the prisoners was a woman and they had cut off parts of her breasts and other parts of her body.

An army captain gave us a very long speech, almost three hours, in which he constantly threatened the people, saying that if we got involved with communism the same things were going to happen to us. Then he explained to us one by one the various types of torture they had applied to the prisoners. After three hours, the officer ordered the troops to strip the prisoners, and said: "Part of the punishment is still to come." He ordered the prisoners tied to some posts. The people didn't know what to do and my mother was overcome with despair in those few moments. And none of us knew how we could bear the situation. The officer ordered the prisoners covered with gasoline and they set fire to them, one by one.

Interviewed by César Chelala
Translated by Regina M. Kreger

Mercedes Sosa
Argentina

Mercedes Sosa was born in 1935, in the Tucumán Province. A singer of Latin American music, she draws from the traditional as well as from New Song. Many years ago, Mercedes Sosa became an inspiration for those who suffer and struggle for justice. She went into exile in 1978, already recognized worldwide as one of the best voices of Latin America. She now lives in her country, but tirelessly tours the world with her music. She has a son, Fabián.

Forced Exile

I was singing in Almacén San José in La Plata on October 20, 1978, while on an artistic tour that also took me to Rosario, Necochea and Buenos Aires.

I felt myself reborn before the audience. Establishing a relationship with my pueblo is essential for me; I listen for their reaction to my songs, filling myself with it to continue living.

This communication compensated me for the "small inconvenience" placed in my way by right-wing groups, and by the authorities, who attacked me for merely singing the songs of my pueblo, songs they consider "leftist," which are, in reality, the fruit of the peoples' pain, their misery, their hope, their work. The poets mold that in words, and we gather their poems in music, so that all mankind recognizes the message of their land, their roots, so buried under the cement of the city and the noise of the workplace.

"Here, We Are the Ones Who Decide."

Not too long ago, I readily agreed to hold a benefit to collect funds necessary to run an elementary school in Lomas de Zamora, a town in the province of Buenos Aires. It was sad to see the conditions of the schools, forgotten by the governments and politicians who apparently had "more important" things to do. Whatever was necessary to continue their operation came out of the teachers' own pockets

The principal of this school asked me to do a benefit which would raise money to cover costs of repairs. I gave my okay and everything was set. But forty-eight hours before the benefit, the authorities called in the principal and asked her if she was crazy. Did she want to ruin her career? Didn't she know I was a "communist"? The woman came to me crying. She wanted to do the benefit at whatever cost, because it was the only way to keep the school open, especially since the province's Ministry of Education was good with "advice" and "threats" but not money.

So the festival didn't come to be, the school probably closed, and the director was most likely declared "unnecessary."

But the night of October 20, another, more serious "inconvenience" would unleash the hate those people have against me, and through me, against everything the pueblo represents. Because, once and for all, what are we if not representatives, ambassadors of our people? When the powerful attack us, they do so because they know that our songs reflect the profound feeling of our pueblo. If it weren't so, they would let us sing even in Teatro Colón*.

So, that night, halfway into my presentation, I noticed "strange" incidents. My agent motioned to me to come closer; at the end of the song, I moved toward her. She offered me a glass of water. Right away, she said, "The police came. . ." So what, I thought; the more the merrier. But the look on her face told me that they didn't buy a ticket, nor did they come to hear me. So I moved closer to the police and asked them straight out: "Can you tell me what's happening?"

"What's happening is that you are singing subversive songs."

"What do you mean, 'subversive songs'? What's that all about?"

"Songs of protest, Marxist. . ."

"But these songs were taped in 1973 and I've been singing them everywhere," I said.

"I don't know what it's like in other places. But *here*, these songs are communist."

"So then, why did you let me get on stage to perform? It would have been easier to prohibit me—and that's it."

"We are the ones who decide what must be done here!"

*Teatro Colón: the most prestigious theater in Buenos Aires.

I thought they would only write a report and cancel the rest of the performance. But the police officers' commands sounded ominous. I thought of one of those Nazi war movies, in which you see the police interrupt a meeting, holding the crowd at gunpoint, and the truth is, *I felt scared.*

All of a sudden, a policeman climbed on stage and started harassing, and I mean grossly harassing, me. I felt so humiliated, enraged. If words could kill, the police would have been dead when I shouted with such hatred: "What are you doing, you shameless cowards!" It was obviously a setup. He was trying to provoke us so that when we fought back they could charge us with "disorder and resisting authority."

They dragged me off stage, separated the men and the women, and boarded everybody onto a bus after ordering all the passengers to get off. Since I was the "most dangerous delinquent" they took me in a police truck. During the trip, the officer who had harassed me moved closer and, ashamed and confused, told me quickly, "I'm sorry, Señora, but it was an order; I had to do it, or else. "

The Tenderness of the Public

We arrived at the Second Precinct Jail in La Plata; Chief Ronconi mistreated us as expected. When I asked for an explanation, he told me that I shouldn't sing any more, that I should stop singing altogether, and he called me "shitty nigger" and other such compliments.

They treated us like criminals; they photographed us, took our fingerprints, and started a file. People were scared; we couldn't go to the bathroom, or speak, or smoke. When one young man talked, the cop punished him so severely that he fell. The kid broke his neck, and was left half-dazed. That scared the cops, who were trying to minimize the incident. I asked them to let a woman with a feverish child go home; they paid no attention.

At six in the morning, the nightmare ended. Slowly, people regained liberty. Stricken, the men started leaving. More animated, the women saluted me, comforted me.

Shortly after that, I gave a presentation in the Teatro Lasalle in

Buenos Aires. Fear took its toll; for the first time in a long time I could see empty seats in the hall. People applauded tremendously, but not so much for my songs. It was as if they wanted to envelop me with their warmth and give me a protective hug. I felt this solidarity, this love, the courage of people who, despite the danger, have come to see me, and I gave myself to the music. I gave the best of myself, forgetting completely the threats.

Weeks later, I had to perform in Cinema Premier, also in Buenos Aires: This time the tickets were sold beforehand, and I arrived at the theater happy, despite the fact that the newspapers refused to advertise the concert and the radio stations wouldn't play my music. I felt happy that day. I arrived at the theater and the people were getting ready to go in when I saw a police patrol: "Again," I thought. But no; again, yes, but in a different way.

"Someone telephoned, warning that there is a bomb inside. We are going to check." They looked for hours. The people were getting impatient; we had to cancel the show, return their money.

What else could I do but leave? They've already bombed Guarany's house. Daniel Chanal, another popular folk singer, was "disappeared*."

And me? I was condemned to internal exile, silence...

Testimony collected by Julio Cardenal, Madrid, February 1981
Translated by Marcela Kogan

---

*On May 21, 1978. The "evidence of crime" found in his house was "a guitar, an artist's workshop, medical and law books, and a lot, a whole lot, of poetry." He is one of one hundred Argentine artists whose return AIDA (International Association to Defend Artists Victimized by Political Repression) has demanded.

Ana Guadalupe Martínez
El Salvador

As a guerrilla commander, Ana Guadalupe Martínez was arrested by the army in El Salvador in July 1976. After being severely tortured, she was released in 1977, in exchange for a wealthy businessman kidnapped by her comrades. Las cárceles clandestinas de El Salvador, *excerpted here, is a testimony and a manual for the militant.*

Secret Prisons
of El Salvador

It was my duty to be silent; I had to direct my thoughts toward the fallen, toward those who had already died seeking to build a new homeland. As I faced each torture, I thought of all the suffering of the people, which add up to something far more painful than what I felt. If I confessed anything, I would contribute to slowing down the process of the liberation of the people.

Added to all this was my worry about a possible pregnancy, because some days earlier, at dawn, Sergeant Mario Rosales, one of our most hated and most cruel hangmen, came to my cell. These visits were so common that it didn't surprise me. This time, however, he arrived with two men, opened the cell, and told me: "Get up and take off your clothes."

"Why?" I asked him. "They just gave them back to me. Besides, I have a bad cough and the cold from the floor is bad for me."

"Take them off, I say," he shouted. "Or do you want these two men to take them off you by force?"

They always sent this Rosales fellow to leave me without any clothes. This henchman must have enjoyed seeing my embarrassment when I started to undress, because ever since I started to take off my own clothes to avoid being manhandled when they did it, he always expected me to.

I undressed slowly. It was very humiliating to me to have to take my clothes off, listening to their obscenities. When I had taken off almost all my clothes and handed them to him, he shouted, "All your clothes. You don't need to keep any on." I finished undressing. What a terrible feeling, both of rage and impotence, when I was naked.

"Leave," he ordered the other two, and straight away he jumped on me like a tiger on its prey, throwing me to the floor. I hit my head and saw stars for a split second, and he took advantage of this to fall on top of me. When I realized what was happening, I began to struggle. I resisted in spite of being handcuffed.

"It won't do you any good to shout because I'm on duty today," he told me. "I'm the one in charge here this week and no one will come unless I call for them."

My cries were choked by the walls of the cell. I tired very quickly. Taking advantage of my fatigue, he called one of the policemen to restrain me, and so he was able to rape me. They were drunk. There was a disgusting smell of liquor in the cell.

Afterward, I thought that the other one would follow, but luckily he didn't, because the second floor telephone rang and they had to go down to answer it. They closed the door.

I remained on the floor, very demoralized, although I had known that this very thing could happen to me. I sat up and saw that they left my clothes in a corner of the room, and I put them on right away. I was aware of every sound, thinking that perhaps they would come back up. They didn't return.

This same sergeant was the one who took people to Mireya's cell—when she was still there—to rape her. They did it several times. They hadn't managed to rape me in spite of all their attempts. From that occasion on, another of my concerns would be that I was pregnant.

Several days later, when my period didn't come as it was supposed to, I became extremely upset, and I was so overwrought that all I could think of was aborting, if I was in fact pregnant. Just thinking about it made me indescribably desperate.

Solitude and silence are also part of the violence with which they try to demoralize and subdue the kidnap victim. Having to see your executioners' faces, without the little joy of seeing a familiar face, or hearing a comrade's voice, make the days more painful and desolate.

That is why, when any murmur of voices reached my cell from the neighboring rooms, I listened to them very carefully. I couldn't make out for certain if they were agents of the National Guard, or the other kidnapped victims who were talking.

One day, at the beginning of my second month in captivity, while I sat on the latrine, I heard Valle, almost clearly, talking to someone. From that moment on, I became increasingly anxious to find a way to talk to them.

During the first week of August, when I was looking through the little hole in the steel plate of my door, I saw Marcelo being taken to the second floor, to be interrogated, I think. That was how I found out that they were holding him there. When they brought him back, I began looking for a way to talk to him.

I was very moved, because after more than a month of isolation, I would have someone to talk to, if I could. I knocked on the wall with my knuckles several times and waited for a reply. There was none, but I tried again, and the third time, I got an answer. Then I found the courage to speak and I called "Marcelo!" several times. Someone replied, telling me to talk louder, and then I almost shouted, "Marcelo!" and Valle answered, "How are you, my friend?"

I looked for the place where the sounds could be heard loudest, near the wall of latrines. If I stood on a latrine, I could hear better, I thought. I did that and then we started to talk, with difficulty at first.

"Hello? Are you all right?"

"And you? How long have you been there?"

And he told me that they had knocked on my wall several times before without answer, and that Marcelo had even whistled, several days in a row, and I didn't hear him, because I was weak; besides, I was lying down, and in that position it was more difficult to hear.

Well, to make a long story short, we began to engage in extensive chats, about the most recent events in our personal lives, but I almost had to shout to be heard. Only when there weren't any guards in the corridor could we talk, otherwise they would tell us to keep quiet and they would threaten us.

Translated by Judith Weiss

Gloria Bonilla
El Salvador

Born in 1951, Gloria Bonilla studied sociology in El Salvador. Gloria left her country in 1981, after her house was raided by the military. She continued her studies in the United States. Her master's thesis dealt with Salvadoran immigrants in Washington D.C., where she works as a legal aide.

Talking

January 4, 1988

I *saw my friend Alicia this afternoon while I was at the post office waiting in line. We began chatting of things, projects, etc. The book, her deadline. El Salvador. Incredible! It has been almost seven years since I left. I have not been back since.*

—Write something, write about your feelings—

It is so difficult to write, to think, to reflect on it. My experience. It is still painful to remember.

I fled El Salvador, leaving behind my family and friends, my undergraduate studies, a job, and all short- and long-term personal goals, in April of 1981 to escape government persecution. In an effort to remain in the United States more than three months at one time, and map out bits and pieces of an unknown future, I was required to change my tourist visa to a student visa. Because the United States recognized then, and continues to recognize today, the government of El Salvador, I have been unable to enter the United States as a refugee, nor can I realistically expect to receive political asylum.

My story does not differ very much from the stories that most Salvadorans tell. I consider myself more fortunate because I did not have to cross the Mexican border and enter the United States illegally. I was also able to maintain a legal status which allows me to continue my education in the United States.

I think, like my parents, I have learned through life quite a bit. My father used to say that we never stop learning in life. He did not go to college. I remember him very much because most of what he knew he had learned on his own. My first recollections of the history of El Salvador were through my father and mother. That history was not in print.

My trip to the United States was sudden, precipitous. I, like many other Salvadorans, finally realized that El Salvador was no longer a safe place to live.

I arrived in Washington D.C. in April of 1981. When I arrived, my good friend, John, was waiting for me at the airport, carrying a heavy coat, assuming I would have no winter clothing. I met John in El Salvador back in the seventies when he was a Peace Corps volunteer. After he came back to the United States, he kept in touch with me, until the political conditions in El Salvador reached serious and dangerous proportions. Then he invited me to come to the United States, an invitation which I did not decline, but which I postponed until I could no longer remain in El Salvador. One day, I called John from Guatemala to let him know I was on my way.

I knew no one in Washington except John, who sheltered me until I was able to support myself. John introduced me to his friends, some of whom are my friends still. As insiders, they helped me to become familiar with the United States. I am grateful for all their help.

A lot has happened since that moment on that spring day in 1981, when I arrived in the United States.

I underwent a metamorphosis. I went from a period of mutiny, in which I encapsuled myself like a larva in a cocoon, to a period of awakening and rebirth. The process was painful and difficult. But I survived. Because I left El Salvador so quickly, I hardly had the chance to reflect on what was happening. When I came to the United States, I carried with me my past, which tied me to people and a land that I had to give up.

There is no medicine to take care of heartache and homesickness — not even here in the United States where there are drugs for almost everything, mostly for pain. I believe we unconsciously or consciously develop methods to cope with those ailments. So, I made up a prescription of my own to help me stay sane and survive in my new niche. I filled my hours, my days, without respite, so I had no time to think, cry or break.

I forced myself to learn English. I took intensive English courses from 9:00 a.m. to 2:00 p.m. I worked in the afternoons. Later, I got a full-time job and I enrolled at the university, finished college and went straight for a master's degree in sociology. I did it all in five and a half years.

I did not do it alone, but with the support of friends. I had moments of despair in which I felt lost, with little or no hope. My driving force was that I had no relatives in Washington to look after me. Therefore, I could not afford to lose my most precious commodity, my mind. Some call it pride; for others it is survival instinct. I experienced both.

The United States Immigration and Naturalization Service regulates, controls, and restricts the free access of foreigners to society and subsequently to its benefits. For example, I had a legal status that allowed me to study and remain in the United States as long as I attended school full time. On the other hand, that same status forbade me to work and compete freely for jobs that I thought I was qualified for.

I maintained that legal status as long as I went to school full time. I paid my bills as long as I worked full time. I had no choice. My constant concerns were basic: food, shelter, education, legal status.

A legal status which allows an immigrant to work is an imperative. In my case, the choice was to apply for political asylum or for permanent residence. The best bet was permanent residence.

Political asylum, in the case of Salvadorans, becomes a dead end since U.S. immigration law requires the applicant to provide evidence of a well-founded fear of persecution. A subjective condition, when you think about it. For example, the army did not need any evidence to determine that I was a "suspicious individual," and to break into my home and my parents' home in 1981. Ironically, it is the same subjective reasoning used by a U.S. immigration judge that determines the non-eligibility of a Salvadoran for political asylum. Salvadorans in exile in the United States have been required to all but present a signed affidavit from their persecutors in order to prove their well-founded fear of persecution.

36

I believe I had good enough reasons to be granted political asylum back in 1981 if I had applied. But a U.S. judge might have disagreed with me, since I did not have concrete evidence of my fear of persecution. Worse, I came from a country whose government is friendly to the United States.

I eliminated the political asylum option from the very beginning. Salvadorans had, back in the early 1980s, little or no chance of having a political asylum application approved; later, it became pointless, since the Reagan administration had invested so much money "democratizing" El Salvador.

I am only an example of what Salvadorans could do if given the chance. In my case, maintaining a student visa gave me access to education, something most Salvadorans have not been able to attain. That is why Salvadorans in the United States hold occupations that require little or no formal education.

I think Salvadorans have tried their best to prove their worth. Our future in the United States does not look promising. Lawmakers had an opportunity to offer better conditions to Salvadorans. The Immigration Reform and Control Act proves it. The United States had a chance to review the law and to review the Central American question, but did not. I believe Salvadorans in the United States have been sentenced without trial. When you think about it, it is not very different from the way our people are treated in El Salvador.

Domitila Barrios de Chungara
Bolivia

Domitila Barrios de Chungára was born in 1937. She had seven children. In 1963, she started to work with the Housewives' Committee which participated in many demonstrations supporting mine workers and the rights of women. Domitila Barrios de Chungara is a survivor of the massacre of San Juan in which hundreds of Bolivian miners were killed by the army. She was also a political prisoner. Her first book, Let Me Speak!, *is an account of her life and a testimony of the sufferings of her people. The book excerpted here,* Aquí también Domitila, *deals with her experiences in exile.*

Two Deaths

More or less by October 1980, I'd received a letter from my sister, Marina. She told me that my children were in her care, asked me to return to Bolivia from Europe, and reminded me of my duties as a leader and a mother. "A leader's obligation is to be with her people, for better or worse," she told me, and that by no means did I have to stay out of the country—but that wasn't my intention anyway. She also suggested that I return in the same way I had returned from Mexico: secretly, because we had a lot of work to do in Bolivia.

For me that letter was a great joy because until that date I didn't know anything about my children, and I felt bitter when I thought of them. Of course in the daytime I couldn't give them much thought— busy as I was, giving speeches and working for human rights—but at night I suffered a lot. With my denunciations and the solidarity work, each day I felt the noose around my family's neck was getting tighter. I'd been receiving threats from everywhere. . .: "You have to remember that your children are still in Bolivia," and so on. My comrades also told me that before engaging in these acts of solidarity I ought to secure myself a refugee status, but I didn't do it. I didn't want my family to have to leave for Europe, and I was ashamed of seeking refuge. Just thinking about it made me feel defeated, no?

After a few days, while I was preparing for a press conference, I received a call from Bolivian comrades in Sweden. They told me they had received a call from Bolivia, that my sister Marina was seriously ill and that I must be prepared for the worst. Of course, at that moment I thought there was no such illness and that my sister was surely wounded or dead—because when someone has been killed, the military dictatorship usually reports: "She died in a lamentable accident," or "He died in combat." And I thought she had been assassinated in reprisal for my activity, and also because she was a leader of the Federation of Settlers.

The impact of that news was so great that I became quite faint. And, as if from a dream, I remember that some people pulled me by the hands, slapped me in the face and wanted me to drink some water.

"Drink it, drink it," they told me. "You have to make an effort, Domi, it's a question of our country, you have to go on with the accusations..."

But all I was thinking of was my sister, and I said to them:

"My sister, my sister is sick..."

"Yes, Domita, we know, but you have to do it for your sister. You have to be hopeful. And we'll finish these projects rather quickly; you must try to communicate with your family later."

Then I went back to the press conference and later went through with the plans for that day.

When I returned to my night's lodging, I was told that I had received a phone call while I was out speaking, and that the caller would telephone me later. But I was so anxious that I begged the comrades to let me call, and I phoned Sweden. There they told me that I must be strong and that my sister Marina had died.

I admired Marina a lot because she was a great fighter.

Just one month and twenty days later, my father died. And a friend told me afterward that he had suddenly aged because he was so much affected by my sister's death, because he hadn't received the letters I had sent him, and because he found out that my children had left for Europe as refugees and he wasn't sure if they had been reunited with me. He even came to think they had been arrested, no?

He died on January 1, 1981 after a slight accident. He hadn't the means for the private clinic. My stepmother took him to the general hospital, but due to the holiday, there were no doctors there. And after waiting all day long for help, he stopped talking, began to snore, and then he died...

Although my father loved all four of us sisters equally, I believe that with Marina and me he felt more fulfilled because he succeeded in having us continue the struggle for his ideals. He was always present at our most difficult moments. He pointed out the way for us, but more than anything he encouraged us to go on fighting alongside the people.

Interviewed by Noema Viezzer
Translated by Elinor Randall

The Russell Tribunal*

An impotent jury

T he Russell Tribunal met to condemn the crimes and violations of human rights against the national native minorities of the Americas. It was a good experience to participate in this jury. I learned about Indian "reservations." It also led me to better understand the sufferings of the national minorities.

The jury was composed of several personalities who listened to the accusations of the affected parties. The idea was that the accused also appear, but since the accused were the self-appointed rulers of the countries from which these national minorities originated, not one turned up to defend himself.

The Tribunal had no power to mete out justice. We could only listen to the accusations, and appeal to world consciousness so it would become clear that in some countries — said to be democracies — many injustices are committed against the natives.

Almost everyone denounced racism, which sterilizes women and imposes an alien culture on their children — they denounced discrimination from the rest of society, no? They denounced others owning the lands they had traditionally occupied. They also denounced religious intrusion.

---

*The Fourth Russell Tribunal on the Rights of the Indians of the Americas, Rotterdam, 1980; named for the philosopher Bertrand Russell.

Among the accusations, which were many, some made a greater impact on me, like those of the Guatemalan Quiché natives. They were represented by two young men who wore masks for fear of repression. They said there were some agents of the CIA and of their country's government in the courtroom, that they were sure they would be killed if they were identified.

They denounced the genocide committed by the Guatemalan army and the assassination of the natives in the Spanish embassy. They said the only survivor of the assassinations had been in the hospital beside the Spanish ambassador; but he, too, was later abducted and killed. The ambassador was told that he would run the same risk if he made any accusations. And when the ambassador left the country, he held that the Guatemalan government was responsible for these crimes.

The Quiché natives demanded guarantees of freedom for their people. This accusation really made an impact.

Another group of natives accused the whites of discovering a uranium mine on their territory, and then taking their lands away from them. They were then taken to work in those mines, and now were dying of some unknown diseases. In accordance with their culture, they had respected those mountains because their gods lived in them; they thought the effects of radioactivity to be a punishment from the gods. They brought films of the zone, of the mountains they considered sacred, and of the people who were dying in the mines. And they demanded that the whites leave them and their gods alone.

The Colombian peasants also made some dramatic accusations. They told about the crimes the natives, especially the leaders, suffered. They said that the Colombian government took their lands away from them and gave priority to the international corporations.

One representative from Bolivia arrived. As the events of the 1980 coup — and the massacre that followed — were still fresh in our minds, there was a great interest in listening to us Bolivians. I don't want to indulge in praising ourselves, but on the day he was to speak, there were more people there than for the other cases. A specialist in native studies spoke from his own position in the racial struggle. He was given enough time. He talked about the culture of the Incas, but he didn't touch the subject of repression. He didn't say anything against the government of García Meza-Arce Gómez, which came to power in the 1980 coup. He even spoke about the Gueiler government (defeated by the coup), and told us that they all had white last names, foreign last names that are enslaving our country. He said that there was no liberation in Bolivia's independence from the Spanish Crown in 1825, that the war is continuing because only one battle has been lost. But since everyone had a limited time, he was told to finish up. He was upset, no?

Then we chatted:

"I support the culture of the Incas," I said to him, "but why didn't you talk about the crimes of Bánzer and García Meza?"

"It's because I didn't have enough time," he said, "and I was waiting for another chance."

And that might have been possible. . . but in the end there were more than forty-five cases to be heard; everyone wanted to talk. And it wasn't fair that some would be heard and others not. So there was a change in procedure. At the start all had the right to talk for one hour; then they were restricted to half an hour; then to a quarter of an hour, and, at the end, to five minutes. Forty-five cases can't be heard in six days. There was an overload of work. We had to stay there until almost midnight hearing, and then deliberating, the cases. We were there until almost morning.

After the participation of the specialist in native studies, we wanted to be given one more chance to finish the accusation. But the Tribunal told us that the Bolivian who spoke had had his opportunity and enough time, and that the only possibility of completing the denunciation was to wait for the arrival of the other Bolivian representative.

The comrade we were waiting for was from the Federation of Farmers affiliated with the Labor Federation of Bolivia (COB). They found it very hard to leave Bolivia, but we succeeded in delaying their case.

I had begged to quit my post on tne jury, arguing that as a victim, I couldn't also be on the jury. I explained my situation and was permitted to act as a witness to the repression, but only for the Bolivian case.

Only minutes before the Tribunal adjourned, the comrade we were expecting arrived. He talked a bit about his organization, focused on the class struggle and denounced what had happened in the military coup — because this comrade had lived through the Army's coup before leaving Bolivia.

Then my statement was accepted as coming from both a witness and a victim. I denounced the fact that I was not allowed to return to my country, and as proof of our repression, I read the "Letter from the women of Caracoles," which denounced the massacre perpetrated by the army in the Caracoles mine in 1980. And when they heard it, there was so much indignation that the people wept and shouted for the guilty to be punished.

One noteworthy thing was that almost all the groups were resentful toward the whites. A Dutch comrade who worked on television drew my attention to this.

"Comrade," he said to me, "I didn't know we had been so wrong. I'm white too, and they're all resentful toward us. But why am I to blame for this thing having happened the way it did? Why so much hate? Why so much rancor toward the whites?"

Then I said to him: "Surely you people must feel uncomfortable It would be good to make the Tribunal notice this."

"Yes," he told me, "I never would have done that to them. I had rather they lived in a just world. That's why I'm engaged in this work, why I've been traveling to make films, to take photographs showing how those peoples live." That's what he said.

The truth is that we felt bad. I had to make people aware that if it is indeed true that the cause of our maladies started when the European whites came to America enslaving, murdering and robbing us of our lands, it must not be forgotten that there are exploited whites and native exploiters. That there are whites who have suffered the same as we did, and they want us to be freed so they help us, no? I noted that fact and some of the comrades laughed a little, but they accepted it.

On the final night we were left alone for two hours to finish up. Our work during these hours pertained to my group, and we still had to listen to four more nationalities. Then the organizers told us to divide the time we had left among the four. But another problem appeared: Four more organizations arrived. They said they had come from a long way to state their problems and that it wasn't fair for them not to be allowed to speak. We consulted about this with the comrades of the first four groups and, happily, they understood. So we divided these two hours among the eight groups.

Among them were the papuans who came in dancing, with their typical dress of pure root fibers. They danced very prettily to the sound of their drums. Then the Kurds entered. When the Kurds took the floor they shouted:

"Jury lady, we want to know how our case is going to be solved. How is the jury going to solve it?"

I tried to explain to them that the jury was only a tribune where one could denounce injustice, but that it didn't have any legal power to oblige the rulers to treat their people better. I told them that we were suffering the way they were, no? That we were victims, too, but that we ourselves had to find the solution in our own hands, and that we ought to unite and struggle for justice. That was what I told them.

Maybe many hopeful people came there. It was some jury! Yes. They talked about their problems. Many of them were able to explain them for the first time. . .

Then a native of the Sioux tribe appeared. He was such a plain person that when I saw him I thought I was seeing one of the Bolivian peasants. His face was withered, his hands wrinkled, no? He approached and said:

"Five minutes, jury lady, I want to talk for five minutes. I've just arrived. I'm from the Sioux and I want to make some accusations, too. Why don't they want to listen to me? Only five minutes," he said.

But at that moment all the time was used up. Then we had to beg the translators. Fortunately, they accepted. It was already eleven or twelve at night. . . He was given five minutes, but I believe he said in three minutes what took some longer:

"I'm of the Sioux tribe and proud of it," he said. "Because my mother taught me to respect women ever since I was a child, because she gave me life. She fed me. My mother also taught me to respect the land, because I cultivate my food from it. She told me to respect the air and not poison it, because the human being lives from it. He breathes. She also taught me to respect the water that ends my thirst.

46

And for me the black or the white or the red does not exist. For me they're all my brothers and sisters. I don't hate anyone. And the same way that I love and respect them, I want them to love and respect me and those of my race, and not to exterminate them as they're doing."

He choked on his words and couldn't say any more. He came and embraced me and said to me while crying:

"Jury lady, do us justice; that's all we ask."

Look, it took him less than three minutes to give such a beautiful and profound message.

Hearing those problems from close at hand has also served to clarify our position as a "jury," which was even a little. . .ridiculous. Hearing testimony, but being powerless to help, is even an embarrassment.

Interviewed by Noema Viezzer
Translated by Elinor Randall

Then who died...?

I n April of 1981, I was invited to Canada by the Committee for Solidarity with Bolivia, a group of fellow countrymen who organized some quite successful activities. My stay lasted for almost a month and a half.

I traveled for the first time with my daughter, Paolita. The comrades had made efforts to pay for her fare; besides, Paolita didn't want to unglue herself from my side. She was still traumatized because I'd left her in Bolivia.

The Committee for Solidarity had reached agreements with the four miners' unions to prepare an extensive agenda. Included was our participation in the May Day march in Montreal. The workers of the four miners' unions were present and it was a very great march. We were told that we Bolivians were the guests of honor.

My little daughter asked me:

"Where are we going, mama?"

"To a march," I said.

And since she still remembered our marches in Bolivia, she asked:

"Just like in Bolivia?"

"Yes. We're going to have a demonstration just like in Bolivia."

But our customs had been different. In Bolivia when there is a march, whether in celebration or in protest, it is done so boisterously. . .with the union band, some dynamite explosions and shouting all through the streets. And my little daughter surely remembered all that. And when she noticed that there was very little shouting in Montreal, that there were none of those explosions she may have been waiting for, after having turned this over in her mind for a bit, she said:

"Mama. Then who died?"

Interviewed by Noema Viezzer
Translated by Elinor Randall

María Tila Uribe
Colombia

María Tila Uribe was born in 1931. A teacher and a political activist, she was arrested, along with her husband, in 1977, and remained in jail for four years. Later, she lived in exile in Nicaragua. María Tila has three children, and is now back in Colombia.

Notes from Inside

I t is not so simple to convey one's thoughts through writing, and I am not a writer. I made myself get into the habit of writing down my experiences in order to relate something about the Colombian prisons and the lives of women political prisoners, as well as my own experience, because many to whom I described life in prison encouraged me to do so.

The subject genuinely interested them. I found among comrades, friends, relatives, and even sympathetic strangers not a superficial curiosity to get a close-up view of something they might know intuitively or guess, but rather a real interest in absorbing such experiences.

I trust that these stories, instead of just being a collection of anecdotes or feelings, can help in creating new and different ways of seeing ourselves and others. I hope that they will be somewhat useful in the struggle to change social relations and will facilitate the establishment of more real and positive bonds between groups of people in order to discover the true meaning of solidarity against injustice in all of its forms.

There is much to tell. I wrote these notes down in any place and at any time, but mainly in the cells. I often sensed the guards' footsteps at night and had to interrupt my work, substituting my pencil with knitting needles.

51

Many women friends assisted me with surprising ingenuity in smuggling my writings out, piece by piece. However, I lost many notes in the final stages of captivity. I myself burned or destroyed what I had written several times because it was preferable to the risks posed by searches.

In compiling and organizing what remained, I have added a few clarifying notes and have removed some interesting episodes which were difficult to explain for various reasons. I have relived four harsh years of day-in, day-out, month-by-month deprivation. I would like to express my special gratitude to my daughter Esperanza, who carried the heaviest burden of this entire horrible prison ordeal, as well as to my sister and brother, Sofia and Juancho. All of those people and groups who offered us heartfelt support, to whom we political prisoners will always be grateful, also come to mind. It is thanks to them and their solidarity—the best expression of their love for the people—that I remember how, I was able, in the solitude of my cell, to imagine hearing tender voices and, instead of seeing frowns, I peeked through the window grates in search of my right to smile.

To smile and to sing—for the confinement, torture, and hospitalization of many women political prisoner comrades were always followed by a smile. Maybe it's because we were made of optimism and hope in spite of being surrounded by sorrows and being so often choked by tears. We women political prisoners, as I recall someone saying, never resembled a funeral procession.

I hope that this testimony is taken for what it is, an expression of hope for a just and dignified Colombia, free of class distinctions and absurd privileges, and an explicit condemnation of barbaric practices, whatever the struggle faced by the protagonists.

. . .I was left semiparalyzed. I was anxiously wondering about what would happen to us and to the children, about staying calm, about a thousand things at once. I had gotten up at 6:00 a.m. to prepare some black coffee. My husband Francisco, the former director of the Technical Training Institute, went out to get some bread. When they banged on the door like they were going to knock it down, I was not even properly dressed. I looked out of the window and saw troops everywhere. The entire block was full of soldiers and army trucks.

Francisco was trembling amidst the machine guns. I saw his face clearly in the tentative rays of sunlight which greeted the morning, just as I saw the arrogant expressions of those who held him, and the frightened people who witnessed the spectacle from the windows facing the street.

Many Colombians would come to know what it feels like to be raided (and thousands more would come to know it during the subsequent government of Señor Turbay Ayala). When asked about it, I remembered that my first impulse was to run away—not out of fear, which in many cases vanishes right at the moment of danger, only to reappear later. I wanted to flee because everyone knows that prison engenders destruction, bitterness, confusion, and melts away achievements and hopes...

I naively went running up to the roof, for nearby I saw the bursts of rifle fire from the neighboring rooftops. When the pounding at the door became louder, I descended quickly to the telephone. What I have never been able to understand is how I dialed the right phone number, to let people know. Then I opened the door.

We were taken into custody...Francisco was pushed straight toward the living room. They shut the door. They looked at me as if I were the intruder. Two, three, four of them came in. One of them motioned to me like a cowboy in a Western, jerking his head up and yelling, "Move it!" while going up the stairs. Many others in the squad passed me. When I got upstairs, I saw them knock down everything that they found in their path.

Then they ordered me to go to the room containing a portion of the library that Francisco had managed to save. There lay the manuscripts of my father, Tomás Uribe Márquez. They were extremely valuable documents for the history of the class struggle in our country, including information about the 1928 Banana Plantation Strike and the subsequent massacre, correspondence with María Cano, his cousin; my mother's letters containing political information, and many other important things of these times.

One of the soldiers calmly began his inspection by taking books and documents down from the shelves, leafing through them or reading titles. He threw several on the floor and the rest out the window into the inner courtyard. He was irrational. You could hear the noise of the books hitting the floor of that patio twelve feet below. The bindings and folders were broken, the pages of documents that had been carefully preserved for years fell like garbage. It had started to rain...

The interrogation began right there. They thought that I had some kind of weapon and tore open my handbag. They demanded "all" of my ID cards, but all I had was my own. Nothing was left after the raid. They took all of the "evidence" and several objects which they liked, even unlikely things such as a framed picture of my grandmother, a little old box with my personal letters, my father's political diary and his study of agrarian issues, things that belonged to my children when they were very young, Francisco's unedited writings, books, magazine clippings, records, cassettes, a small alcohol stove and the mattress. They destroyed our home, but not the unity of our family which, although we were separated, always remained intact.

Four hours later they moved me to an army base at Puente Aranda. I agonized over the fate of Francisco, who had stayed behind with the soldiers at the apartment. When we said goodbye, I cast a fleeting glance at him; possibly he was thinking of my fate. We exchanged quizzical looks, but each was absolutely certain of the other's stance.

During the ride in the jeep I thought: The city is deceptive. They might have followed us a lot without it being obvious, or someone might have "made a deal" leading to our arrest. And now the soldiers were going to score points for it.

But I, having this false sense of security that is so dangerous for those who dare to think and act against the powers that be, told myself: eight days and my situation will be straightened out; this bad time will have passed. What an illusion! For I had not yet experienced what it means to be in the hands of military "justice."

All of this happened on the day following my arrival in Bogota. It was March 24, 1977.

After the meticulous paperwork, the humiliating and threatening glances and comments from several individuals, they locked me in a room. I calculated that it was 2:00 p.m.: they had also "seized" my watch. Interrogation began in that room. They came in one at a time, hooded; I did not rest for three or four hours, as they themselves noted.

Thus I spent the day, that night, the following day and...I lost track of time. Only later was I able to figure out that this interrogation lasted until the following Monday. I remember that at some point I saw the light fade into the distance, or I fainted, overcome by exhaustion—they would bring cold water to throw on my face—and I also remember a voice that would wake me up: "Get up! The captain's coming!" I asked how long I had slept and the man told me: "Two hours. You've slept quite a bit."

With no food or water, the hunger you feel the first day is not the worst of it, nor the sick feeling that follows, nor the vomiting at the end. Most worrisome is controlling your nervous tension in the face of threats and provocations. Especially when faced with the worst poison: "the good guys" who project trust, demonstrate "friendship," and pretend to understand and, indeed, identify with the ideals of justice. A large percentage of denunciations and frame-ups, of incriminations and self-incriminations result from the work of the "good guys." They come to "save" the prisoners from the clutches of the "bad guys." They are experts in adulation, playing on one's vanity, giving one the benefit of the doubt, and manipulating interviews, combining lies with true statements. In my case, this was the *modus operandi* of two of the interrogators.

I saw the first enter with his hand at his waist, corpulent in the shadows of the room. He was wearing a black leather jacket. He had a soldier bring a not-very-large cardboard box and put it on the small table; the soldier then left. He locked the door and approached, with slow, heavy steps, the only chair in the room, leaving us face-to-face; I was sitting on the bed, and the table was between us.

Others had already been through, always hooded, always jotting down my responses in their notebooks.

Through the holes in the hood I caught a glimpse of something that inspired fear: the hole for the mouth revealed large teeth, reinforced with gold above and on the back side, which I gradually discovered the more he shouted at me.

There were two main lines of questioning: where was my son Mauricio? and who was participating in the literacy work?

He began by emptying the contents of the box on the little table, some fifty small portraits of my son, all identical.

"Where is this son-of-a-bitch? You can send word to him to give up peacefully. We're going to go after him. We already know where he is. We're going to bring his corpse right here, *right here!*" he shouted, pointing to the floor by the door.

He continued in that tone, insulting, questioning, threatening. I felt my blood pressure rising and my patience running out, since I was making a great effort to say nothing in response. He stood up, he sat down; then I pulled my gaze away from his eyes and toward the pictures. I took one, thinking of keeping it. I held it in my sweaty hands, and at the same time I was frightened by what he was saying, horrified at the thought of my son as a corpse. It was as if I'd seen that same photo in the newspapers, like the portraits of the dead. Even though I tried to rid my mind of such thoughts, I kept imagining my little boy dead.

"And whose son is that son-of-a-bitch?" He kept talking to me, shooting off questions like a machine gun, denigrating me, humiliating me in a way that is only done by those who falsely consider themselves to be "superior." Men with a sadistic attitude toward women, especially if the women are political prisoners, like to show off their ability to insult the women in their own characteristic way: "vagabond!" "bitch!" "trash!" The scene was brought to a high pitch with shouting, aggressive attitudes, and insults, until he threw all the pictures to the floor, repeating: "We're going to go after him, you'll see, very soon you'll see."

I don't know if he was trying to make me react violently, but it happened to me only that one time. I jumped up, overturning the table, shouting at him: "Go ahead, go ahead you wretch, but go alone. Don't send troops, *coward!*"

"She's crazy," he shouted. "That woman is crazy." By then he was near the door, and the others came to see what was happening. They observed the disorder, and saw me in a rage. Then they all left, leaving me locked in, tired, as though I'd just run a marathon, frightened by the threats, feeling desperate. I held my head, and breathing heavily, I said aloud, "Wretches, what more do they want to subject me to?" Then I got hold of myself, realizing that since I'd kept control earlier, had I continued showing my pride, then it would have given them more reason to finish me off. Several times I truly thought that the end had come.

The second interrogator opened the door very quietly, a few minutes later, and in an even quieter voice began to tell me lies as he approached: "My God, what has been going on here?" he said, looking at the mess. "Why are you so upset? Who did this to you? Please calm down, señora; let's talk. Would you like a cup of coffee?" It was the first time I ate or drank anything.

"No, I don't want poison. Please leave me alone."

"Don't worry." A soldier came in with an elegant coffee tray. The interrogator served the coffee and had some himself.

"Now you have some. If you want to rest, lie down."

This was how the "good guy" technique began. Talking for six hours. . . Measuring my words for six hours, uninterrupted, like in a verbal chess match. And he went on telling me about his life: that before he had lived in Cartagena; that it was only recently and by chance that he came to work as an interrogator here in Bogota; that I should trust him and ask whatever I wanted to know. And indeed, I asked if in his work in Cartagena he had met an exceptional prisoner, Mother Herlinda Moises.

"Oh, yes, of course, I was talking with her," he said. And was it true, I asked again, that they let loose a dangerous snake in her cell?

"Uh," he answered, "well," as if it were the most natural thing, "yes, but it was a small snake, nothing that would scare anyone." When I refused to give him information about my son, asking that he understand that this would be impossible for any mother, his tone changed a bit. It was then that he removed from his folder several sheets with information related by Mauricio's university friend, whom he — as I had in the past — admired for his intellectual abilities and good judgment.

"Good judgment," he said, "this man, fluent in several languages, also has good judgment! Read this yourself, convince yourself that to refuse no longer makes any sense. He is one of the top-ranking men, one of those in charge."

I read it. At first I thought it was a trap, for they could put anything before my eyes. I reread it. I then realized that it was a detailed admission of his revolutionary activities, a denunciation of many people.

At one point he even went beyond the interrogator's questions, saying: ". . .and to give you more details I'll tell you the following. . . ."

And that had repercussions beyond his interrogation. His

words, and over time the repercussions, remained in the file. If I note this, it is not to pass judgment on him, as I, too, am a human being.

I do not have sufficient criteria to answer that immense *why* that I cannot explain for myself. I speak of this situation because for me it was *too painful*, because it was torture to deal with it, and because the "good guy" didn't need to say anymore to see me cry in silence, gritting my teeth. That alone, though it was not my defeat, was his triumph.

The interrogation ended with him offering to get messages and papers to my family, to intercede on behalf of my health, to remove the extremely strong light bulb from above me, to give me food and drink...But I did not believe him, and he failed to keep his word.

However tragic a situation, at some point humor inevitably intercedes. An interrogator told me he was a student at the National University, that he was very familiar with, indeed was an expert on, the student milieu. At one point—the session lasted over three hours—the following dialogue occurred:

"Who inspired that literacy work?" he asked.

"Necessity," I answered.

"I mean, who actually contributed to make it work? If you collaborate, everything will change for you." The Major says that here the troops also need to learn to read and write, and "since you like that... imagine, it could be a job for which you could charge as you wish. Think about it, and collaborate. Who made those primers work?"

"Well, to a large extent, Paulo Freire. We also learned from others."

"Who else?"

"Anibal Ponce."

"Who is he?"

"He's an Argentine."

"Do you know him?"

"Not personally."

"Can you describe him?"

"No."

"Then, how did you learn from him?"

"You know, from his message. . . He wrote — " He abruptly cut me off.

"To whom?"

"To many people." He continued taking notes in his folder.

"Is he a communist?"

"I think so."

"And you still deny that you have foreign ideologies and that you are directed from abroad. Where is he?"

"He ended up in Mexico."

I should note that my intention at the outset was not to tease him. I wasn't up to it. But the mistake left me an opening, which I decided to take advantage of. That's why I laconically commented on Ponce's life and work.

Of course, I was tired and I didn't want the confusion to drag on long. So I asked that we leave it for another day. A bit bewildered, he stood up, gathered together his papers, and said he would return. Henceforth I was scared by what I had said, but there was nothing I could do about it. Naturally the denouement came. You can imagine the most unpleasant things when it came back to me, threats in retaliation for the deception, and the desire for revenge felt by him and another interrogator. But I couldn't help but laugh when left alone, for I deduced that they would go look for Anibal Ponce at the National University in Bogota.

When they removed me from the cell, I walked some four hundred and fifty feet across the lawn of the Brigade of Military Institute (BIM) headquarters; from there you can see many beautiful buildings. The building where I was taken had only offices. It was noon and the typewriters were quiet; there were only three or four men around. They took me to a rather small room, whose walls and ceiling were covered by thick black cloth, with intense reflectors in the corners of the ceiling. They ordered me to look at them; naturally I couldn't, since the light hurt my eyes. They gave me the orders through a speaker, I think, in the ceiling. Of course in such a small room it's impossible not to notice where the voice is coming from; but I was in such bad shape, and moreover, I was very frightened. Locked in, I tried to gaze at the door handle the whole time, to see just when it would be opened. That's what I was scared of.

I waited, frightened, for them to come in and mistreat me, while the voice ordered: "Face the mirror" (attached to one wall), "Turn toward the door! Look at the right reflector!" Then another voice began to interrogate me, threatening me with what could happen to my children if I didn't collaborate.

The heat radiating from the reflectors and the lack of air in the room made me sweat all over, and I only had a small handkerchief. Following prolonged silences were more instructions, questions, and threats. I responded to the instructions, and questions; in a faltering voice I responded to the questions with: "I don't... know; I'm... not aware." I responded to the threats with silence. To give myself strength, I pretended that many eyes or faces of *compañeros* and friends were accompanying me, to protect me; it was only a matter of convincing myself, while time passed. The last silence continued for a long time. I thought they might have left for a while. And then the door opened and I saw a man. At that moment I shouted, *"No!* Don't torment me any more!" And I thought of my children. The man ordered me: "Out!" Outside, in the office adjacent to the room, another man, with a tape recorder in hand, told me: "We are going to take a sample of your voice; read this." And he handed me the text I was to read. It was about the maintenance of arms and how to use them. I saw the time on his immense wristwatch: ten minutes to two. I realized that I'd been in that black room less than two hours, and I was happy to have my wits about me. Perhaps that gave me courage not to act like a robot reading something that could be used against me later. On top of the desk was a newspaper, so I grabbed it and began to read. "No!" the man with the tape recorder said. "Read the text!" But I had the guts to refuse. "If what you need is a sample of my voice, any text will do," I said, and I continued reading until he cut me off. "That will do," and turning to the other man, he ordered, "Take her away."

I returned along the same path to the interrogation room; the shadow of my body on the floor was somewhat longer than on the way there, when the rays of sunlight had come straight down.

Inquiry

The judge, civilian in appearance, but with the spirit of a military man, was in his office, located in another building of the BIM. I found him short, chubby, white, and greasy. It made me uncomfortable that he didn't look me in the eye when speaking to me; but at unimportant moments, when I was distracted he glanced at me.

When he read the arrest order for "conspiracy to commit crimes," he named seven crimes, taking for granted that the charges were a *fait accompli*, or so it seemed to me. I was so surprised that I couldn't let him go on. I interrupted: "How is this possible? What are you telling me?" With a soft voice he responded: "Don't get so upset, señora. As you prove your innocence, we'll erase them. They've been listed collectively, not individually." Ignorant of legal matters, I could not answer; I did not recall the universal judicial principle that everyone is innocent until proven guilty. I also forgot that in an arrest order a judge can say what he wants — in this case to instill fear, confuse me, or entangle the process. What is true is that charges are only valid once they are proven. Even more true was that as far as this judge was concerned, the law wasn't worth the paper it was printed on.

The inquiry was brief. I had only one regret: the certification of "good treatment" that he left for me to sign. I hesitated, I didn't know what to do, because of my ignorance regarding these matters. I thought that after the inquiry there would be more interrogation, and thinking that it might be worse if I didn't sign, I decided to do so.

That certification is used as a precaution, in case the accused later says that something he or she said was extracted under torture. This was not so in my case; but they later brought many such certificates before international organizations.

With the inquiry, the first stage of my time at the Brigade headquarters came to an end. I did not see the interrogators again.

Francisco, who was also taken there, had outdoors recess at the same time as I did. It lasted an hour, and so we saw one another sometimes. We would walk along a paved area; and though we were being watched, we could talk. Extremely concerned, we would meditate on what to do. Meals became more regular. My younger son, daughters, and siblings took turns on the short visits permitted on Wednesdays. Almost all of them realized that on leaving they were followed. I spent more than forty days like this, forty days of fear, bitterness, uncertainty, and anger, such as the night when I heard the terrible cries of a woman, never knowing who she was; and all Francisco was subjected to, very worrisome because of their twisted intentions. I cannot forget the punishment I witnessed being meted out to a soldier on the lawn by a sardonic and miserable official who, whip in hand, forced him to behave like a dog; the humiliation to which my family was subjected when coming to visit; their tears when they saw me there.

I remember the soldiers' frightened faces, their looks of sympathy and quite telling attitudes: offering me water, turning the light out at night (which was prohibited), dropping a newspaper with apparent carelessness when bringing meals, leaving me a sweet taken out of a pocket. And I remember the judge's indifference vis-à-vis my requests to confront my accusers before him, because he must have assumed that they would have been in my favor. And as for the official in charge of the political prisoners, I remember his power.

We hoped to be taken to legitimate prisons, because we thought we would find relative security and rest — also relative — from so much tension.

They came for me one day out of the blue. I couldn't say goodbye to Francisco — they wouldn't let me — which left me feeling immensely sad. When I got in the vehicle that would take me to the women's prison, I was feeling hopeless, discouraged. I asked myself: how long will this go on?

Translated by Charlie Roberts and Vladimir Klimenko

Women and Prison

When speaking of women in Colombia, and the innumerable circumstances which torment, condition, or deform them, it is imperative to mention the prison population. Official sources give a figure of 8,000 nationwide. Stated plainly, this percentage is not very disturbing, almost "natural." But statistics are often like a mirage. Let's look at reality: We are talking about 8,000 convicted women who are part of the full-time prison population, who, on the average, serve two- to eight-month terms, besides the relatively small number of those given long sentences. In other words, no fewer than 40,000 women pass through the prisons annually, not including those who only serve several days, spending their nights in smaller municipal jails or police stations. A number of detainees arrive here as well. They are released quickly, as if by an act of magic. One of the most tragic consequences is the way in which thousands and thousands of children are left without adult supervision.

Along with political prisoner *compañeras*, we have been analyzing the general discrimination against women, the specific discrimination against women in confinement, and the discrimination which we ourselves, on an individual basis, have felt throughout our lives. It is obvious to all of us that one important motive in our struggle is our passionate desire for a change in the social structure which would permit us authentic personalities. We speak about the ugly machismo, this monstrosity which demands submission to a man's will, whether a father, brother, boyfriend, lover, son — even a grandson. Almost all of us feel angry at ourselves, because to some degree we have helped stimulate this evil, despite our belief in our own political awareness.

In confinement, I come to realize that almost all of the women ended up here by depending on a man. In other words, although there are economic factors behind crime, with few exceptions, it is generally men who make decisions, give instructions, and administer things.

I have seen cases of political prisoners whose involvement arose not out of political awareness, but out of their desire to be with the man of their dreams. With the passage of time, they developed a political awareness that they lacked at the outset. The reverse also occurs: a woman fully understands what her role should be, but cannot develop her abilities because some male authority figure stands in her way. In that case she must make a break away from him. She does it in order to progress, although at some cost to her emotions.

In any case, sexist discrimination takes on even greater force in prison. This is not only because women are seen as lesser beings by their families, their relations, their employers and others, but also because institutions like the courts have placed women in inferior positions. Over the centuries, laws have been devised and approved exclusively by men who represent oppressive state institutions which are the primary source of inequality.

Discrimination is more tangible here. It is seen in the crime of "abandoning one's domestic responsibilities," the penalties for abortion, the brutal violence of male guardians, and abuse by certain male authority figures. Men may be allowed two visiting days, with more hours, and are allowed a conjugal visit. Meanwhile, sexual abstinence is imposed upon women as if we aren't human beings (or even animals).

Those who are here for having left their households are among the millions of Colombian women (married and unmarried) who have been formed — or deformed — exclusively by the "obligation" of having to perform domestic labor like servants. Too poor and too busy with husband and children to obtain any training, they end up convincing themselves that they are incapable of anything else. They see their only option as being dependent on and, of course, subordinate to their husband. Women who leave their homes are especially justified by the enormous tragedy of their lives, their lack of education, and the absence of support.

One woman who should never have come here married a molester without knowing it. She had a daughter by a previous relationship. She had a premonition when she observed the stepfather's "strange" attitude toward her daughter; she took her little girl and left. The "abandoned" man filed a legal complaint and gave the judge explanations which may or may not have convinced him. And since she had neither witnesses nor proof, she was jailed for two months pending the court's determination of the truth.

This occurs quite often. Sexual abuse of the wife or her children is quite common. What turns out to be exceptional in this story is that she not only suffered his insults, lived in a state of anxiety, and was pommeled by life, but also, by being married according to Catholic tradition, she facilitated her husband's sending her off to jail.

In the last cell in this dark corridor is another young woman here for the offense of leaving her husband; this time for adultery. The abuse she suffered from her husband and his girlfriends did not matter; that's why he is a man, said the judge. Nor did his coming home in a drunken state matter. She found herself attracted to another man, maybe because she was tired of hearing herself called a whore by her husband, and having to dodge his blows after his drinking sprees. She decided her fate by leaving and ended up here for that.

All of us know the double standard which one must submit to and even respect. It requires a woman to live by rules which do not apply to a man. Until a few years ago, this woman could have been sent here for adultery, a cruel statute for infidelity under which only women were punished. Colombian legal history is full of crimes in which the victims were women accused of adultery. The defense pleaded "anger and intense sadness." The husband thereby regained his "honor" and retained his social reputation as a macho and upright man worthy of respect.

One sensed a sincerity in the woman in the last cell. However, she had to resort to unnatural hypocrisy and lies, given the high price demanded of her by a *machista* society. In order to avoid challenging conventions and laws, she would have put up with years of being obedient, silent, "virtuous," domestic, submissive, and pure toward her virtual master. And, like millions of Colombian women, she would also be assailed, reviled, offended and humiliated during her lifetime, and then recognized as a saint after her death. The saints made possible traditional marriages at the price of sacrifice and maintaining appearances.

Legally prohibited and morally censured, abortion has for years been the subject of periodic — and useless — debate between representatives of the state and the Church. The problem has still not been resolved. Those who carry the burden on their backs like red-hot irons are the thousands of women who need a solution. For otherwise, abortion remains a hidden tragedy which, besides physical damage (aggravated by the lack of medical care for over seventy percent of all Colombian women), causes psychological problems and, as if all of that were not enough, carries the risk of imprisonment.

Here one often sees women who arrive sick and infected. The last one was taken to the hospital, but it was too late. She died.

There also exists a group of cases, seventeen to be exact, of domestic employees (an exclusively female domain) who came from the countryside. They are not paid and time passes; the employer promises to pay them later, in one lump sum. But one fine day, jewelry, clothes, or other valuable objects "disappear." A legal claim for theft or robbery is filed and while the case is investigated, the judge sends them to prison.

While it is impossible to know whether the accused are guilty, we do know that most are released six months or a year later, almost always innocent. They are women who have no experience with the courts, no money for paying lawyers, and who do not have enough education to defend themselves, even verbally; they have only the hope that some kind soul will speak on their behalf. When released, they can register no complaint, and for the rest of their lives are stigmatized by their status as ex-prisoners.

The immense rural exodus of peasant women to urban centers goes on uninterrupted; lost in the large cities, many seek work as servants. One might think they could work as servants until the day they die, but for a variety of reasons domestic service is disappearing from the social scene. These women tell stories of their parents abandoning their lands because of Liberal-Conservative violence. Those who have come to the cities in recent years note that in the name of "law and order" and the war on subversives, large businesses are set up, yielding huge profits, in the countryside; of course neither they nor their family members are involved in such businesses.

Peasant women suffer more than city people in prison; they are discriminated against not only for being poor and female, but for being peasants. One of them said: "Had I been allowed to choose who I was to be at birth, I wouldn't have chosen to be a peasant." Another added, "nor a woman." I have heard city people (in prison and outside) say that peasants have a hard time realizing the crisis that is their lives, because it is a continual crisis; or that since they don't know any other lifestyle, they neither long nor strive for a better life. Perhaps such people have never thought about why so many peasants abandon their lands. Such statements are contemptuous, as is the belief that only those who have had schooling and intellectual development can think and feel, that others are "dense."

As I listen to them, it seems as though I am a spectator who understands many things differently. I accumulate a great many impressions, and I feel things which, I believe, may be of interest. For example, submerged in their tragedy, marginal women rarely see the economic or socioeconomic causes of their degradation and crime. They almost always attribute their situation—because they've been taught to do so—to free will, innate evil, cruel fate. Almost all of them say that when they came to the city they looked for work in factories and shops, that they have even, in some cases, landed factory jobs; they've been barmaids in low-class bars, vendors of knick-knacks, beggars, unemployed. It is at that point of desperation that they are initiated into thievery, relating to the scum of society, or that they fall into the hands of pimps, who sell them. That is why many end up combining prostitution with crime.

In theory, prostitution is prohibited in Bogota. That is what makes it operate at this level of destitution. Aged before their time, exposed to venereal disease, fatal abortions, and alcoholism, these women put up with contemptuous treatment, are seen as immoral, and are persecuted by nightly roundups. They may spend hours in a dingy prison cell, be released in the early morning after having been beaten, watched while dressing, and insulted by the same men who in other circumstances are their clients.

Another direct tragedy women suffer here in prison, since they are women, is the termination of sexual relations with their male partners, which in our society just makes the man feel all the more justified in setting up a home with another woman. According to the women affected, their depression, crying, and anguish, feelings of total abandonment and disillusionment result from sexual abstinence. In addition, there is the ensuing tragedy for the children. This is a very common topic of conversation here. During the Sunday visits you can witness women trying to have sex with their husbands, partners or lovers.

In the infirmary, I saw a young woman knitting baby clothes, not speaking with anyone, staring only at the needles. She had just emerged from a gynecological exam. The nurse ordered me to enter just as the pregnant woman was leaving. She passed by, and I noticed she was someone who had been in prison for two years. I then had my turn with the same doctor, a woman, who had been appointed as the assistant to "Doctor Aspirin."

The doctor, in contrast to the prison staff, acts human. She knows that my problem only requires one consultation, but she also knows what she represents for those of us who live here: someone who comes from the outside world, tells the news, listens, and gives us strength to go on. Since she is leaving soon, she does not deny me these conversations, which for me are a time for easing the day-to-day tensions of prison life. After a friendly greeting, I noted:

"That young woman. . . pregnant. . ."

"Disturbing, isn't it?" she answered. "She's the third case I've seen in the three months I've been here."

"But is it possible? She's been locked up for two years. . ."

"You haven't seen other cases of psychological pregnancy?" she asked.

"*No*! I haven't heard of that. What does it involve?"

"It stems from sexual abstinence, in addition to some other circumstances. . . the repressed desire to be with a man, with her man. It becomes obsessive; at night she imagines being with him, and she lets her fantasy run wild. Masturbation, you know. ."

"Unfortunately," I told her, "It's discrimination; in the men's prisons, conjugal visits take care of this. But here..."

"And the disorders are manifested quickly," she went on. "Women have come to me to have the objects they've put in their vaginas removed. Sometimes. They don't consider the danger... It's depressing, don't you think?"

She continued explaining what for her was of scientific interest, telling me of "symptoms" such as vomiting, menstrual problems, even swelling of the abdomen.

"Then... knitting, making baby clothes, preparations, looking for a name for a boy or girl. Finally, three or four months later, the disaster! The woman has a 'miscarriage,' all imaginary, as you can see."

One of the consequences of the lack of conjugal visits is an increase in lesbianism, which is prohibited and punished, tolerated or encouraged, depending on the whims of each new director. The absence of a clear policy creates confusion resulting in psychological problems.

Officials try to subdue prisoners with "rehabilitation" sessions. After such sessions, women who did not attend always ask, "What did they say?" The invariable response is: "Bullshit!" Rehabilitation sessions are also occasions for discrimination, even from such high level officials as the National Director of Prison Rehabilitation.

One case was a rehabilitation session at which attendance was compulsory. The major in charge of rehabilitation began by threatening whoever might try to leave the auditorium; he asked the prison authorities to write down the names of anyone making funny gestures; and when he felt he was in command of the auditorium, and the sighs and coughing were suppressed, he came out with the following: "What can the children of imprisoned women grow up to be? What, but prostitutes and pickpockets? You think you can make peace with God and the homeland some day, but only think about seducing guards so you can give birth to more children. You leave the prison, and you look for someone to bring evil to... and instead of making a decent home you throw yourselves into bed with the first man who propositions you."

However low in the social structure, no one has the authority to humiliate an audience in this way. There was indignation, murmuring, and more hatred. He ended up by promising sports fields of all kinds, and he spoke of setting aside "land for building you a swimming pool," in a place where there are no trash cans, the receptacles for kitchen waste and dishwater are disgusting, the walls are falling apart, no one is given a toothbrush, nothing is kept up, and where you breathe only misery.

Translated by Charlie Roberts and Vladimir Klimenko

América Sosa
El Salvador

A mother of seven, América Sosa became involved with the Comadres — the Mother's Committee — after the kidnapping of one of her children in 1980. In 1985, she left El Salvador to escape repression and to represent the Comadres in the United States. She moved to Washington D.C., from where she has traveled extensively denouncing human rights violations in her country and in Latin America.

A Mother's
Testimony

July 1987

The majority of Salvadorans want to stay in our country, for it is what we know. Before coming to the United States in 1985, I had a life that I felt good about, a permanent job, even though the government and the army were persecuting the people, especially those who work for human rights. I was feeling happy about my life and my work with the Comadres. Before 1980, I had not been engaged in this kind of work. I was dedicated to my seven children, my husband and my job. I worked in a factory and, during my free time, I participated in the Christian community. I was really busy, and I had no intention of leaving the country.

In 1980, my fourteen-year-old son was captured as he was getting out of school. I sought the Comadres for help. After some time, we were able to locate him with the police. He had been sent to prison without a reason. My son did not participate in any kind of political activity. His life was dedicated to his studies, but because of his youth, he was an easy target. Young people in El Salvador are always suspected by the authorities. After my son was freed, my husband was captured, in 1981. He was physically and psychologically tortured, which was probably the reason for his death. My husband was taken from police headquarters to the hospital because of his wounds. It was at that point that I became more active in the Comadres. I had a reason to participate when my family was directly affected.

The Comadres have been persecuted by the army, and many of its members have been selectively harassed. Many times I had to move from my home because I felt that they were watching me. So, every four or six months, I was moving with my children in order to avoid capture or the injury to my children. In 1984, when the mothers were invited to Washington D.C. to accept the Kennedy Human Rights Award, four of our members were chosen to travel, but the State Department denied their visas. We were told that we were a threat to the security of this country. So it was difficult to come here legally. No organization in El Salvador could help us come here, because the work that needs to be done is in El Salvador. Only one of our *compañeras*, who was touring South America, was able to attend the ceremony. She participated in public gatherings and press conferences. The award, which was really visible here in the United States, recognized the mothers' work for human rights in El Salvador. Because of this, the North American public became interested in supporting the mothers' work. Many churches and humanitarian organizations wanted to collaborate in a more practical manner with our work. We received an invitation for one of the mothers to come and work in the United States, but this was difficult because we didn't have the government's support.

I was chosen to come to the United States because I had been very active and committed to the work. Since I couldn't come legally, they told me: "We need you to work there, for about two years or maybe one, depending on the situation." I never really thought of coming to this country, to learn about its culture, its problems, its politics. When we hear about the United States we think it is a paradise, don't you think? We think it is the most beautiful country, the best in everything, the most free. . .we think of all the fantasies that we see in the movies. We contacted our friends in the solidarity movement, and in the churches, to help me come to this country with some kind of security so that I wouldn't get stuck on the road, or on the river. I was helped by the people in the sanctuary movement, who were already working hard for the protection of Central American refugees. I was able to meet very kindhearted people, who are very committed to the sanctuary movement, and who have become the main support system for the Central Americans who are in danger in their countries.

I was in danger in El Salvador, but I am also risking a lot in this country because I am speaking publicly about the politics of the government of my country, the role of the army and the role of the American government in El Salvador and other countries in Central America. Because of my work, I still need the protection of the churches and the people who are engaged in this project. But, sometimes, it really bothers me that people come and ask me why the Salvadorans stay in this country, when they could stay in Mexico. Other people say that we come here because of economic reasons, that what we want is to work and earn money. At this moment, eighty percent of the Salvadorans in this country are people who are escaping the war and who want to avoid the political insecurity of their country. Not only economic reasons lead us to leave the country, but, of course, we can't deny that there are economic problems in El Salvador, and that people can't live from air, don't you think? We all need to work. But in the case of the Salvadorans, the economic problems are not the main reasons why we leave. The main reason why we come here is the political, social and military situation in El Salvador, a situation that is similar in Guatemala, Honduras and Nicaragua where the people are being attacked by the contras. We can't deny that we are political refugees in this country. We are war refugees because there is a war in our country, a war between the Salvadorans and the U.S. government, which is sending military advisers to conduct the political and military war from the U.S. embassy. The U.S. role in El Salvador gives us more reasons to stay in this country; from here, we can try to find a way to solve our political and military problems. The situation of the Salvadorans is critical. It is clear that the U.S. government is giving priority to Nicaraguan refugees, instead of paying attention to the situation of the Salvadoran refugee. For them to acknowledge the Salvadoran situation is to accept that they have made a big mistake in our country. They are not willing to look for a peaceful solution to the problem, but instead follow a military strategy.

The Salvadorans are denied refugee status—yet why does the United States provide that status to refugees from other countries? The Angolan, Polish and Afghan refugees are immediately given political refugee status. It is obvious that in our case the United States is avoiding its responsibility in the Salvadoran war.

What we, the Salvadorans, want is the solidarity of the people of North America. They must become aware that the problem of El Salvador is not an eight-year-old war, but a fifty-year-old conflict of social injustice and economic inequality. It is the problem of a small minority that controls the wealth of the country and a majority of 90.8 percent of the population that endures exploitation and misery. . .The military comes and crashes any effort for justice. This is the real reason for the war. It is not what the government calls a "communist problem." In my forty-nine years, I never met communists in El Salvador; I don't even know what communism is. Since 1932, we have been constantly accused of being communist; 30,000 Indian campesinos were massacred because of this. . .We seek international support in order to achieve self-determination and national dignity. The North American people should be aware of this reality and help us find a peaceful solution to the massacre. The massacres committed by the army and the security forces must end. People are looking for a new way of living, but they are not allowed to work for change. Many North Americans have been thrown out of El Salvador because they were providing food to people who were being relocated. You don't have to throw bombs at people to kill them; there is another way of killing people — to starve them to death.

There is a real danger that the war can reach other parts of Central America, because of the pompous policies of this government that day after day become more aggressive. . .Many people will continue to be killed. More and more North Americans will be killed as well, not only the blacks and latinos, but also the whites. The first months of 1987 were proof of this. How can it be explained that a plane full of military advisers, flying over a war zone, would crash because of "mechanical problems"? This is evidence that the war is not only killing and mutilating peasants and children, but also killing military advisers. There is no reason why these people have to go to our country to die. That is why I always say in my speeches that the Salvadoran war is really the United States' war, since they are directly participating with their military advisers, their arms and their money. The U.S. citizens are sending their money to El Salvador to kill innocent people. Why? What's the reason? What benefits do the American people get from the war, other than shame, discredit and the horror of reliving Vietnam? People here know that many Vietnam veterans are either crazy or lost. They didn't find meaning in life after coming back from the war. There are many who are not in favor of war and have become peace supporters. We want to reach those North Americans who are conscious of justice and peace. We even want to get to those who are ignorant, who don't know about their government's policies — and I'm not only talking about Ronald Reagan's policies. I'm talking about the institutionalized policy of intervention and exploitation of the countries of Latin America; the policies that make this country richer while Latin America becomes poorer, as it acquires a huge external debt that we will never be able to pay. This country should understand its proper role in Central America, South America, South Africa and the poor countries of the world. . .

We Salvadorans should be left in peace; we could be far more effective as friends than as enemies. We don't want to be the United States' enemy or, for that matter, anybody else's, but we definitely don't want to be invaded. It is our right to demand self-determination.

Interview by Adriana Angel and Natalia López
Translated by Natalia López

Irene Martínez
Argentina

Irene Martínez was a medical student when the military kidnapped her in Argentina. She was tortured and spent time in jail and under house arrest. Irene lives in exile in the United States, where she practices medicine and plans to specialize in the rehabilitation of torture victims.

A Visit to
My Mother

I t happened many years ago. It was a very warm winter. July, the sun
was bright, the air fresh, transparent, pure; even some birds were
singing. However, I couldn't feel happy. My body was heavy, numb,
and tense. My head was spinning; I was trying to breath slowly and
deeply, like in a yoga class, to relax. It didn't work. My voice was not
my voice; I wasn't myself, I wasn't there, another person walked for
me. Finally the bus came. "A ticket to Belgrano, please." I deposited
my body on the front seat, right behind the driver.

"Sir, would you please let me know when we get close to the
school?"

"Yes, señora."

"My mami has been working there for five years but this is the
first time I take the bus to see her, you know?"

"Yes, señora."

After the big turn we left the paved streets. The bus jumped. My
numb and tight body shook like a bag full of potatoes. Even though I
tried hard to concentrate, I couldn't remember the night before. What
sound had really woken me up then? It had happened at 3:00, the
right time for "the others" to come. The shadows that hit homes. But
it had been him. Pale, tense, he had whispered in quick words.

"They, the shadows, visited Sara's place. They only looked for
her. I was there but they covered my eyes and left me lying on the

floor." Then he left and I had gone back to bed. At that moment, I realized I was not myself.

"Here's the school, señora," the driver's voice reached me. I got up, slowly, with difficulty. I walked off the bus, landing on firm ground. I walked into the school, entered the principal's room and asked for the second grade teacher, my mother.

"She is busy now, you'll have to wait until the break," the secretary told me, and left the room. I felt like screaming. I wanted to tell her that that teacher was *my* mother, that she was first my mother. I felt angry and jealous. I hated all her students, the same way I did when I was a child and I couldn't have her at my school during the festivities because she was with her students. Oh, how I hated to share her!

I walked to the central square, that brown and muddy spot called the "patio." Nobody was there; the wind lifted the dust, and I could hear the noises, laughter or silences coming from the classrooms.

I heard the bell, and one minute later she showed up. My mother, the teacher, in her light blue uniform, her pockets filled with pencils, pieces of chalk, papers, scissors. Her hair short, uncombed, her face with that eternal worrisome expression, that face that can light up and change so much when she smiles. That time there was nothing in her face, not even surprise. "Hola," she said, "what are you doing here?"

"I came to say hello; well, I really came to say goodbye, mami. From now on, for your own safety, for mine, you can't know where I am or what I am doing. I won't go home any more, at least for a while. Last night they took Sara, and I don't know what will happen next. The police and the army deny having her. I hope she is alive."

My heart was pumping so hard that I could barely hear my voice. There was a silence, the air became dense; her voice got through.

"That is not possible! What do you mean? I must know where you are, I promise I won't tell anybody. I need to know if you eat, sleep, if you are safe. . .You can't leave this way. . .and what should I tell your father?"

"Mami, you can't. This way is better, don't you understand?" I was using up my last drops of energy. "Listen, I'll call you. . . I'll let you know about me. I'll call you to find out about the family, to see if there is news, if they went to look for me." Words sounded sharp as knives. "I must go."

Silence. No air. No sound. No laughter. A terrible smell covered us. The acid smell of fear. I kissed her and left. I don't think I hugged her; I didn't turn my head. My vision was blurred, but there were no tears.

I had to keep going. I left her in her light blue uniform in the middle of the brown spot. How did she get to the end of the school day, how did she teach her classes, how did she sleep that night and other nights? How did she cover my absence? What emotion did she hold in her chest after I denied her the right to her daughter and gave her, in return, fear and uncertainty? I don't know. I have never asked you, mami. What happened to you during all the years that followed that afternoon? Because, after all, those dark shadows found me and took me away from everything, as you know, mami.

II.
That Story Burning Inside...:
Narrative

Marjorie Agosín
Chile

Marjorie Agosín teaches literature at Wellesley College. Among her publications are two volumes of poetry and several volumes of literary criticism. She is also a journalist and has strongly denounced human rights violations in her country and in Latin America.

The Blue Teacups

November in Stockholm. A light and delicate darkness slowly surrounds the city, as if little by little the wide and angular sky were beginning to prepare for the great polar night, a night of an immense and greenish sun.

The lights of the city begin to wither with the grace of an agile ballerina and, in the twilight full of veils and nostalgia, appear the candles of generous spirits surrounding the city and a light that invites the peace, so strange and desired, that can only be achieved through silence and the night.

In Stockholm, I begin to become part of this magic and rare luminosity. I walk through alleys that seem to be populated by the goblins of Nordic legend, so alien and yet so familiar, because among all the blond heads and this great and heavy silence, it is difficult to feel like a stranger. At times, I walk hurriedly; other times, I slow to contemplate how a thin hand reaches to light another candle, in a bare window, populated by crowns for ancient queens.

A small candle placed at the end of the street calls my attention, and I am overcome by an overwhelming need to climb the stairs of the illuminated house, to pound on the door as if a distant voice calls me. Nevertheless, I must remember that I am far from my Latin America, where, despite the disappearances, the pains and daily kicks in the stomach, we still dare to enter a neighbor's house with the sole purpose of passing time.

The candle seems to mark the route of my pilgrimage; its undulating fragrance pleases me in this darkness of goblins and, determined, I begin to ascend the staircase that calls to me, naive, astute or wandering, daring to dance, sleepwalking, smiling, responding to the call.

I discover that I have arrived at a wake. There are no bodies, only belongings. The women who are usually spectators at births and funerals secretly hang old tapestries on the bare walls. They hide the broken shoes of the dead woman and, as if enchanted, they clean some blue teacups with golden edges.

They are some of the most beautiful teacups I have ever seen. I ask myself, could they have belonged to an elderly woman presiding like a queen over a family drawing room? Or, could they have belonged to a forgotten spinster caring for the vestiges of her family and her own loneliness?

I stop to contemplate the cups; they are as blue as the ocean or my grandmother's eyes. They remind me of bodies that, after making love, shine with desire. They smell of travel and elegance, and surely belonged on a table of golden wood, or at least were bought at a pawnshop at the end of the war.

I do not know whether I should ask about the history of the blue cups or better to learn from enigmas of that which is unsaid, to simply be or allow oneself to be taken by this dignified elegance. I discover that the cups belonged to a Jewish woman from Hungary, and that they are from distant Bohemia. They tell me that, above all, the woman never let go of her teacups and that, in times of leisure and happiness, she contemplated them.

These teacups hold the stories of so many exiles. They have traveled, have been buried before and after earthquakes, and have survived the loss of children and homes. I do not stop observing them, and it seems that in looking at the blue cups, I find myself with my eyes full of the roads of my great-grandmother Elena, the one who, one morning, had to leave her house, her feather pillows, her histories and her memories because she was Jewish. She could have been Moorish or black, but nevertheless was obliged to abandon the territories of her geographies. She carried with her her bronze padlocks and crossed the Atlantic and the Pacific until she arrived in the port of Valparaiso in

Chile, where she planted flowers and found a new wall to hang her keys.

Now I bring the blue teacups from Stockholm to Boston. They seem like the veins of lost children that search for the familiarity of smiling faces or a piece of bread on a friendly table. The blue cups are in my home, I care for them and love them because, in them, I preserve the waters of so many exiles. The exile of the woman from Bohemia who, before dying, must have left me the message to care for her most precious memories. I also imagine them in the home of my grandmother in Vienna full of fragrances and bits of orange. I will never know the true history of the blue teacups. Perhaps someone will come in search of them and will return them to their true home while I look at them, celebrate them and love them.

Luisa Valenzuela
Argentina

Luisa Valenzuela was born in 1938. She started as a journalist at the age of seventeen; four years later, she published her first novel. After the 1976 coup in Argentina, her works were blacklisted by the military. She settled in the United States where she had previously lived. Luisa actively denounced the human rights violations committed by the junta. She has published three novels, several collections of short stories and many articles. She has just finished a new novel.

On the Way
to the Ministry

There's a certain terror when one says "present" and suddenly discovers that one is absent or one's mind is somewhere else entirely. It's not at all easy to move ahead through a reality bristling with nails: on putting one foot down after another with the greatest caution, one must immediately lift one's foot up and hobble along and is no longer present here and now, unless one is a fakir, which one isn't.

A fakir he is, though. He's been practicing for years to say "present" and put his foot down hard as though corroborating the word. There are more and more sharp nails in the streets and that makes him happy; he can leave everyone open-mouthed and, taking advantage of people's amazement, secure a public office. His years of hardening the soles of his feet have also let him make a detailed study of the habits of officialdom. He now knows that it's in moments of maximum astonishment that vacancies come about, hence the need to fill the posts with new people. (He isn't burned out, if one takes the word in its metaphorical sense and not literally, because he's successfully undergone the test of fire and many others.) He has everything planned: he's going to leave his house with firm footsteps and walk in a natural, almost martial manner to the Plaza, where the carpet of nails is thickest and most bristling. There all he'll have to do is wait — standing on the nails — until a policeman with heavy boots comes over to him and offers him a job. (He'll stand on the nails thinking about the nails: perhaps they've been put there to justify the boots, which otherwise would fall into disuse, what with the new technique of electrical prods.) He'll have to choose the rush hour, perhaps two in the afternoon or when the banks close, so the amazement at seeing him pass by with such a determined step will be really efficacious, an apotheosis. He hesitates between coming out of his house barefoot — something too eye-catching, almost vulgar — or wearing light moccasins with no soles like Indians. He opts for the latter and as he waits for two or three pairs to be brought out (he must anticipate wear and tear, in case he has to repeat his exploit), he continues his daily exercises to toughen the soles of his feet: a half hour of number three sandpaper, a touch or two of the soldering iron, walking on thumbtacks scattered about the house. He no longer feels any pain as he walks, but his stumbling doesn't yet have the grace necessary for him to be named minister or even secretary. He continues to engage in more and more fruitful practice, and with success so close at hand he doesn't regret the long years of sacrifice necessary to arrive at this point. His political vocation was always so heartfelt that he was not going to disregard it out of the mere desire, for instance, to keep a wife. Graciela left him in the third month of training: You were unbearable when you ran the country by talking in that committee with your coreligionaries, she claimed, but you're a thousand times worse now, spending all day at home mistreating your feet. I hate masochistic politics. Goodbye.

He merely smiled at her with a certain hidden scorn and so believed that he had saved his pride, even though he'd lost his beloved. You'll regret it when I'm minister. You'll come crawling back to these very same feet that you scorn now, but it'll be too late, he answered her, even though it was too late for this sentence since she'd already left, slamming the door behind her. In the beginning he was sorry that his wife had left, but the years of apprenticeship and monastic life had made him gradually abandon any earthly aspiration. The desire for power was the most ardent of all his desires, therefore we now find him full of inner peace, involved in the final preparations as he awaits his moccasins that will pave the way. The desire for power has become almost a burning passion with him. The neighbors wonder what the burnt smell is that emanates from the house of the quiet, lonely man, almost a saint. In the beginning, as he carefully burns the soles of his feet with a blowtorch to form a protective crust, the smell is as faint as the smell of meat cooking. Gradually it gets stronger until it becomes almost unbearable, because to the smell of his burnt feet is added the burning ardor of his uncontrolled desires. Even so the neighbors don't lose their esteem for him — a man so thrifty and modest — and just think, since his wife left not a bit of laughter or even a little music or any of the other things that usually bother neighbors has come out of his house. He sets an example for the whole block, even though his house is far from being the most neatly painted or elegant one.

It doesn't seem possible, but in this world everything eventually comes out, and the news of the grand march that he's preparing for, stamping on the nails, has reached the ears of the neighbors, and they are anxious for it to happen. An anxiety that, because of the smell, turns into anguish. They begin to fear that he has given up his ministerial vocation and devoted himself, body and soul, to a mystic one. To think that they've all been patiently waiting for him to be named to his post so as to ask him for a nice cushy job in some official agency, or a promotion for their son who works at Customs, or an unpretentious little pension. In their hopes for a helping hand from him, all these years the neighbors have unselfishly ministered to his needs, leaving a pot of food at his door — the spaghetti left over from lunch, a bit of fruit, a special treat on Sundays or holidays, and *mate* already made. This has been a daily practice so he won't forget them when the moment comes, and also to keep him healthy until that moment.

And now he has taken this detour by way of sanctity and they (the neighbors) feel swindled. He eats hardly any of the food they bring; on the other hand the food they bring now isn't so fresh, and they no longer care about his caloric intake (if he isn't going to be a minister, he doesn't need to be well fed or well groomed, so no more soap or shaving cream or expensive deodorants either). He doesn't even notice these lapses, just as he never used to notice their attentions: he quite naturally took them to be a logical tribute to his constancy and the profound political vocation that made him a hero and a martyr.

The neighbors call for a hero, but *he* is inclined toward martyrdom. Ah, what will become of us if after so many preparations this man doesn't rush through the streets, disdaining the nails and causing general stupefaction, to get himself a ministry! He now has every chance of resounding success (they say during their less frequent neighborhood meetings), yet he's tempted to throw it all overboard and choose another path. Our informants say that he's still preparing for the Stupefying March to the Plaza, but what if he's decided on some other strategy? Perhaps in the rooms at the back of the house where our hidden cameras and microphones don't reach, he's preparing himself for altogether different activities. The burnt smell that comes from his house is thought-provoking. They are almost certain now that he has given up his plans to be a minister and has embarked on a useless spiritual quest. When all is said and done, a man capable of spending several years preparing to act like a fakir might well become interested in something more secure and lasting than an official post. Eternal salvation, for example.

"And why doesn't he take us, too?" the neighbor who's shrewdest at making long-term investments asks at the next meeting.

"Why not indeed?" the other neighbors chorus, convinced that they deserve something for having taken such good care of him through the years.

And that is why, as he waits for his moccasins (a month at the most, he's been told), he finds a great quantity of candles and white flowers at his door instead of the food. His thoughts run more to a change in diet than to a step from the material to the spiritual world. The candles, repugnant even when cooked in a stew and indigestible in the bargain, pile up in one corner of the kitchen, but the flowers are edible as a salad. A few days later hunger makes his stomach growl but fails to assuage his burning desire for power. He gets his hopes up on the morning when he finds an enormous grill in front of his door, because he doesn't know that the neighbors have thought of Saint Lawrence on account of the burnt smell. He dies with one image imprinted on his retina: that of the spare ribs that will allow him to try out the grill. For more than a week the neighbors continue to leave flowers and candles outside his door. They think that the new smell coming from the house is the smell of sanctity that they've heard so much about. And they finally feel entirely rewarded for their efforts.

Translated by Helen Lane

Alicia Dujovne Ortiz
Argentina

Alicia Dujovne Ortiz was born in Buenos Aires and has lived in France since 1978. She was a columnist for the Mexican newspaper El Excelsior *and wrote for* Le Monde. *She has published three collections of poetry and three novels. She has allowed us to excerpt her unpublished novel,* Vamos a Vladivostok!, *which is a search for her own roots, a narrative of the lives and adventures of her ancestors that, surprisingly, begins with Columbus' travel to the New World.*

Courage
or Cowardice?

The one who dreams up tests, practices, experiments. He sits in
front of the fireplace and throws in sticks. Let's see what
happens, he thinks, if I throw in a dry stick, a fat one, or a narrow
green one. Each new story is like a burning stick which, when placed
on top, changes the position of the rest, because it takes in the heat
from those below which, when they feel its presence, stretch with
anxiety and stick out their tongues to try to trap it.

The linden trees were humming in Moguilev-Podosky in 1890. It
was the bees in the trees that hummed, although even a careful observer
would have believed that the sound came from the whirlwind of leaves,
spinning like tops, falling like the twirling locks of the Hasidim.

The stocky, green-eyed man, looking much like a gypsy, with long
eyelashes and heavy eyebrows, arranged himself on a park bench in
front of the synagogue, watching the leaves fall as if he, himself, were
going through each and every one of their little deaths.

On another bench, a skinny blonde watched him watching.

After a while, he returned from the horrors of his small abysms
and saw her.

"Sara Brun!"

"Samuel Dujovne!"

Then she looked into his eyes with the same look he had while
staring at the leaves:

"What's wrong, Samuel?"

Samuel picked up a leaf and moved to the blonde's bench:

"You see? The vein holds only the center of the leaf. That allows it to fly, it flies doubled. It's a divided creature. Until now, it was a simple leaf, like any other leaf. But from here on, and without warning, one part of it gets loose, changes its course, as if saying 'let's go—' but..."

"But what?"

"Can't you see, it's the 'let's go—' of suicide."

Sara turned red with anger. She was a woman with fine, pale skin whose blood rushed to her head in a fit of rage. She told him to quit joking around, that the leaf flies off to propagate, and to find in this otherwise natural gesture a reason for sadness was...was... Indignation choked her.

Unexpectedly, Samuel moved closer to her and whispered in her ear:

"Then, let's go."

The blonde understood. This triggered something inside her and she stood up. Mindlessly, she kicked around some leaves and took a deep breath:

"Are you serious? Would you leave?"

"What can we lose?"

Exasperated, she sat back down. She burst out, that wasn't the answer: one doesn't go to the Hirsch Colonies in Entre Ríos, to the south cone of the world, only to bitterly shrug his shoulders.

"Each person reacts the way he can, Sarele," he murmured.

Sorry for her outburst, she tried to make it up to him by egging him on, testing to see if mouth to mouth resuscitation would spark some light in the big, sad eyes of the leaf-watcher:

"Do you know how many each settler will get? Three hundred hectares."

"It must be thirty."

"I'm telling you, three hundred."

She told him again that she was in Kishinev where the conference was held by that Baron, the French gentleman who wanted to save them from the pogroms and that, yes, three hundred, because the Argentine pampas were expansive, barren. She repeated "plains," repeated "endless" with such gestures of greatness that to stop her from flying off he kissed her.

Was he kissing her? In this life most kisses are not meant for the lips of lovers. In Sara's lips, Samuel kissed Argentina, and not, as she said, out of any faith, no, not out of faith, but out of an image of white feathers that floated through his mind.

(For the Jews of Besarabia, the days after Czar Alexander II was assassinated turned into days of white feathers. Samuel couldn't remember the blood or the wild screams of the pogrom. He remembered ripped mattresses and hands cutting into them looking for treasures. He saw a huge knife tearing into his own little mattress, and beautiful snow, fluttering in the house as in a music box.)

He removed his lips from the feathers and he said, fearfully:

"I don't want them to give me three hundred, Sarele, I wouldn't know what to do with them."

She pushing him on, lobbying him:

"There isn't a Jew who knows. We'll learn. We'll return to the land, Samuel, we'll free ourselves from the intellectual chains, we'll work with a plow and sickle. . ."

He turned pale.

"How would you expect me to liberate myself from intellectual chains?"

And she, totally fed up:

"Ay, Samuel, Samuel! Now you'll tell me that for centuries you lived stepping not on land, but on books, not on paths, but on carefully chosen words, Hebrew, Arabic, even Sanskrit; you'll tell me you have gypsy blood, and that you read somewhere that gypsies live in India, and that's why you study Sanskrit; you'll tell me you call yourself spiritual, but, I can't take it anymore. Samuel, I can't take it. Wake up, because that's not what life is about!"

Her fiance looked at her as he had looked at the leaves, as he had kissed her: turned inward, looking into himself, kissing his own ideas, he sighed.

"Don't you feel that life keeps redrawing a drawing that's already on the page? Look: let's learn Spanish. When the Jewish minister of Califa of Cordoba learned the Jewish kingdom existed in Caucaso. . ."

"Look, Samuel: if you don't wake up, I'm going alone."

He picked up his teacup with the silver handle, the one the

Christian crowd couldn't find in his mattress, looked at the reflection the light made on the red liquid — as if rubies were dancing like gnomes. What other choice do I have? he thought. The four old men were waiting for the school teacher to give a speech about their hopeful future. The old men listened from far away, daydreaming, their eyes and ears in the clouds that were white like feathers:

"The Baron of Hirsch...a colony waiting for us in Entre Ríos...the Jews born in Argentina will need teachers...enough tales, I'll finally be able to tell them that Moses took advantage of the low tide to cross the sea...Argentina, the land of promise...enough pogroms...a terrain to sow our ideas...ideals of teaching...take part with the growing of a new nation, what a present from history! The teachings of Pestalozzi* growing like wheat."

They dressed in gloomy black: He wore a black hat, she a dark kerchief. When they saw each other dressed, they didn't recognize one another. There is a certain type of dress, more than that, a certain posture that defines that kind of farewell. Immigrants and the dying all look like a brotherly troop, knowing that they will never return. They share the resignation of forgetting their own names. From the moment they left, they knew that nobody would call them *Dujovne* with the exact accent over the "e." Like you wave a fly away from your face on a hot, muggy day, they were already waving away the certainty that they would have to explain for the rest of their lives that you pronounce it *Dujovnie*, not *Dujovneh*, with the sharp, awkward Spanish "e" that would finally impose itself...

Then the frisky horse trotted over the snow. And the bells rang with a prolonged echo, an echo that still resounds in the ears of those who need to hear it...*Don't leave...Wait a while*...Don't take that iron train, don't deprive those who come after you of the massive snow over which people travel by the sound of the bells.

Other Dujovnes had traveled to form a Hebrew tribe in Entre Ríos. They left lighthearted. For months they had to fight the Zionists, the Bundists, who told them: "I'll spit in your face." They spit in their faces because they were wasting their sweat in a foreign land, or because they escaped just when Russia was preparing its great revolution. But

---

*Pestalozzi: Swiss educational reformer, 1746-1827

this little group of Dujovnes, tired of national homelands and bolshevik outbursts, escaped from Besarabia, from the pogroms, and from the Baal Shem Tov, and the Black Sea, and the Caspian Sea. . .ran away because "fear is smart," as they would quickly learn to say, when they started to drink *mate* with their matzah, instead of tea.

A Russian Jew who boarded the train or the boat in Odessa, and then went through the zones the Czar prohibited Jews and gypsies from crossing: anonymous Jew. In the land of gentiles, neither Bundists nor Zionists, nor even pogroms, disturb families, only the colorless and enormous wind. They shivered under their long gowns, but not from the cold. Arriving in Marseille, the shivering was gone. But not because of the heat. Now, in this port they discovered that exile takes away one identity and gives you another. All immigrants looked alike. They were small, all bow-legged, all dark, all wearing long, black coats. Has anyone even seen immigrants with slim, graceful figures, dressed in beige, wearing hardly anything, their legs naked as if they did not fear? That would be hard to believe: the destitute travelers cover everything, from head to toe. Lighter colors undress them. Olive-colored and short, the women tried to hide their large asses, which they gained by eating cornmeal, *varenikes*, spaghetti or lentil stews. Only the rich deprive themselves of the grains that the unfortunates seek as a homeland to console themselves. . .On board the boat, Jews prayed, rocking back and forth. The movement of the sea quadrupled their motion. A heretical Portuguese mother was breast-feeding two rather grown children. Once in a while, they interrupted their routine to vomit over some phylacteries and talit, which at one point were white, but had since been abandoned by their owner, who at least had the decency to vomit into the ocean.

From the dark brown river, Buenos Aires faded into the pampas. "We're here," they said.

But where? Together they trotted in packs; legs tired, long gowns disheveled, they reached the Hotel of Immigrants. From the windows they could see a city with slate roofs, like in Paris, with windows adorned with metallic bars, like in Spain. They could see buildings topped by green domes and small statues of gesturing cherubic women, like in Italy. . .

Days later, they woke up in the station of Palacios, Entre Ríos, with its ornamental edges and fragile columns, like in England.

Under the eaves stood a small group of gauchos. Dressed in boots, *bombachas and facones** slung across their backs, their hats shading a familiar expression.

The gauchos turned toward Samuel; because he was the teacher, he spoke some Spanish...

Samuel stroked his beard, straightened his overcoat, fixed his hat, futile gestures because afterward he bent over, picked up a handful of Entre Ríos dirt, kissed it. He then spit out in Spanish:

"How are you my friends?" That made the group burst out in laughter.

He thought he heard a word in Yiddish. But he was determined to hear only a strange language. Familiar sounds passed by him. Nonetheless, the sound came back. Could it be? He uncovered his ear. Yes, the gauchos with facones and bombachas were saying in Yiddish, welcome home.

"Jewish gauchos!"

"What are you doing with that huge coat, Don Samuel? Hurry, man, keep that hat on if you want, but put on your bombacha—you aren't going to hobble the cow dressed in clothes of mourning!"

"Hobble the cow," murmured Samuel. "In Russia, the cows plant themselves, ready, to be milked. The cows live with the people in the house, they practically greet you in the afternoon while you have tea. Where in Monguilev would you ever have seen a cow so ornery as to wait till the pail was full to kick it?" He stood watching her, thinking, Yes, it's a cow. But it's not a cow. It had a furious, stubborn expression. Cow without love. American cow, cow of a solitary land.

"And the horses?" he continued. "Every Russian horse knows when it should stand so the owner can put on the harness. Here, by the time you get to the pasture, lasso an animal and yoke him to the cart, you forget where you were going. And, in the end, the snorting devil takes off several blocks ahead, and then slows down, trotting at a short pace that, now that I think about it, reminds me of a Turkish horse, only they're a little smaller and have more hair."

---

*Trousers and daggers

"Don Samuel, the plague!"

He had barely put down his bundle the morning of their arrival, when one of the first things they said was: "Locust." Assimilated Jews from Kiev, from Kishinev, all on horseback, wearing facones informed him that, as a teacher, his most sacred task consisted of fighting the plague. He would teach Jewish history ("Moses took water from a stone because he discovered a stream flowing underneath."), arithmetic, Argentine history, Spanish (when he gets to speak it) and locust. Damn bugs! They left their eggs all over the trails; you recognized them as you would a clam bed at the beach, by the little breathing holes they poked in the earth. Don Samuel, and his students, went after class to remove the dirt with shovels, hoping that the eggs would die when aired. But if they didn't die, they got jumpier; the larvae grew and formed a thick carpet. . .land seemed to be moving. . .Don Samuel was getting dizzy. . .The other settlers, more patient, cut of a different cloth, went out on horseback, dragging a hollow can to sweep the moving mass, pile them in little mountains and burn them. The blazing balls smelled like fat frying, crackling loudly. "The way corn bursts when you make popcorn," said a red-haired gauchito; his mother called from afar:

"Moishele! Careful with the fire!"

But the locusts! Sara was sweeping the dirt and manure floor, when she was captured by a rising darkness. Is the storm coming? No, the storm doesn't buzz. When she went out, she found her husband contemplating the cloud that was blackening the sky, and murmuring:

"I've asked myself when the next pogrom would come. There it is. Sarele: here the Cossacks don't ride horseback, they fly."

"But do something, you idiot, *move*," she roared, pulling the sheets from the bed to shake them like flags of truce. Everywhere, you heard the sound of cans, pans frantically struck by spoons like a band of street musicians playing without rhythm. The contrast between the playful gestures and the reason for the banging was tragic. Quickly, the trees where birds sang, and the patches where flowers grew, and the sky blue area covered with alfalfa as tall as a person: All pure memory. The snakes that hid between the stalks were left naked. Iguanas, giant rats, hares, partridges, foxes and weasels were catapulted from the straw into the air. . .

Nothing remained, not even a thistle patch. It was hard to believe, but neighbors, arriving by horse and carriage from Rajil, Rosh Pina, Espindola, San Gregoria and even Domínguez could swear to it. A rough thistle five meters high, which used to be parted with machetes to clear the path from one farm to another, was reduced to skeleton. A cow was killed. Gloomy vultures glided in circles each time getting closer, until they attacked the animal, devouring the eyes and udders.

It was the first time he said it. And the first time Sara answered him:

"And you? What, are you going to kill yourself! You don't have the courage."

He stopped to think about it. Casually, as if concerned with an ethical question rather than inflicted with suffering, he asked her:

"Do you think you need courage or cowardice to commit suicide?"

"Courage," she said, again making the beds with the sheets defeated by the plague.

But when she returned to lay out the feathered quilt, she was curious.

"Kill yourself, for what?"

"Because the pampas are too large."

By the afternoon the dust was in the air. A short raging wind followed... Suddenly, in the green sunset, the sky cracked open. "The lightening looks like a coral snake," said a poetic farm worker who had smelled the storm coming and decided to stay drinking *mate* and eating matzahs with the Moishes. At first, drops of warm water hit the earth and poked holes in the ground. After that, the dams of heaven broke loose. For heaven's sake! yelled the farm worker when a wind swept the roof and stones fell on Saul's crib, scarring him for life.

"The same thing happened to my brother, when the white feathers — " said Samuel. "Do you know? Here the pogrom is natural: it's not of man, it's of elements."

"Stop it, Samuel."

By dawn, the hut was destroyed and the pampas turned into a pond with muddy worms as thick as fingers and as long as arms. .

"And Sanskrit, Samuel?"

"Well," he shrugged his shoulders. "There must be some gypsies in Entre Ríos. But to tell you the truth, I'm not so eager to find out if some elements of Sanskrit remain in their language."

On the wall of the school that the wind hadn't taken, Samuel hung another portrait next to Pestalozzi: his new idol, Sarmiento*. In the drawer of the yellowing desk was his hand-written letter from the Baron: "I highly recommend this young wise man who will raise the cultural level of the colonies." That was also losing its urgency. The pampas made urgencies fly away. They lit the candles to celebrate Shabbat, yes, they lit them every Friday night, every Rosh Hashana, and Succot and Shavuot they would repeat the gesture. . .

In 1903, Carlos was born. He should have been called Akiba because, in the tidal movement of his ancestors, it was his turn to receive that name.

"Akiba, Akiba," repeated the father, thinking, "Mmmm. . ." According to tradition, three men descended to the kingdom of the shadows. One returned crazy, the other blind and the third, Rabbi ben Akiba, returned home healthy and safe, saying that he had found himself.

A moment of doubt, and then:

"No. I couldn't do that to the poor child. Why give him *Akiba* to screw up his existence in Argentina! Better give him a name without history. Something lighter. Something that sounds similar. Sarele, Sarele, let's see, what sounds like that in Spanish?"

"Carlos," Sara said.

The same year they received a letter from Kishinev.

"My dear nephew," grieved the old woman, "we've had a tragedy. Your father Leon died in the pogrom. Couldn't find words to tell you how hard it was, and I can't even remember it very clearly because all I could see from my hiding place was an immense amount of white feathers. You must think I'm crazy. But the assassins ripped open the mattresses' bellies as well as ours. Somebody told me that Leon died right away, without suffering much, but I didn't see him, I didn't see anything, because of the feathers."

The second time that Samuel asked if suicide was courage or cowardice was when the ceiling flew away. The third, when the letter

*Sarmiento: Argentine president, one of whose priorities was public education.

arrived from Kishinev. Shortly after, the family abandoned Carmel Colony, because the pampa was too large.

They rented a room in a poor boarding house of Cordoba, whose windows had a certain colonial air, and for a good reason: there had lived Viceroy Sobremonte, of whom people sang during the British invasion:

At the first canon ball from the brave
Sobremonte and his family escaped

Does running away take courage or cowardice? In Cordoba, Samuel sold soda bottles, opened up a bakery, and began meticulously feeding the fruit of his death. His three children turned into average Argentines. The fourth, Carlos, the one who should have been called Akiba, but was spared the name, became a founding member of the Argentine Communist Party and, at the age of eighteen, went to the USSR, whirling, gyrating like a leaf that returns to the tree. . . Did Samuel ever think that the true gift of history wasn't in Argentina, but in Russia? And that the young Bundists were right? Did he think about that? Sure. Bitterly. It's easy to guess his thoughts, you can almost hear him chewing on them, desolately chewing on them, night after night. . .

It was 1930. Back from the USSR, Carlos was living in Montevideo, presiding over the South American Bureau of the Red Organization of Trade Unions. Suddenly his old man comes to visit. He did not look old, he looked transparent. It was possible to read through him, through his nose and his fingers. . .The effort of focusing on only one thing for so long made him look like what he thought about: he and his question were like those old married couples, or like those people who live with the same pet for fifteen years. Together they swayed, swinging at the same pace, he and his question, together they reached a perfect clarity, an air of clearness, of intellectual neutrality. But this time, Samuel Dujovne traveled specially to Uruguay, to pose the question to his son:

"Tell me, Carlos, you who are a communist. What do you think? Does suicide take courage or cowardice?"

"Cowardice," Carlos said, who, at that time, thought about it.

He returned to Cordoba. How long was he there? The time needed to ask the last question.

"Courage," said Sara.

She won. He went to the room next door and fired into his body a shot that echoed infinitely. Somebody can still hear the prolonged sound. If that person of strong memory was asked about Samuel, the answer would be that Samuel is the legend of a thoughtful man who meditates on his problems, examines every angle, and finally resolves them.

The one who dreams us puts pieces of wood in the fire to test. He blows. He suddenly notices that he can blow more fire in one place than in another. As if, there, in that spot was a wound, which he keeps fanning until the sore becomes a flame. The flame that must pass, forcefully, to a new piece of wood.

Translated by Marcela Kogan

Cristina Peri Rossi
Uruguay

Cristina Peri Rossi was born in 1941. She was a literature professor and fiction writer in Uruguay. In 1972, she was expelled from her country and moved to Spain. Cristina Peri Rossi has written four books of poetry, four collections of short stories and a novel. She lives in Spain, where she works as a journalist.

The Influence of Edgar A. Poe in the Poetry of Raimundo Arias

I've behaved, I swear it," said her father, looking straight at her. His eyes were the clear blue eyes of a small child. Later in life eyes darken. Alicia had observed that characteristic of eyes. Something in life cast shadows on them. They lost that color of a lake where geese can contemplate their own reflection. The quiet waters shook: internal currents coming from afar, from other horizons, from overseas, changed the rhythm and tonality of eyes. Then, children were no longer children, turned into men of dark eyes, men with no eyes to mirror anything. It became impossible to look inside as she could still do with her father's eyes. She liked to lean out on those waters. She could see sand dunes, marine animals, stones, bright spaces and the serene yet disturbing lunar geography of the sea. If he stopped being a child she could not look into his eyes and see the dangling Hippocampus navigating slowly, or the white-flowered plant with the golden stalk. She blew on the plant and the stalk moved. Her father closed his eyes.

"You've come back late," she said in her clear soprano voice, "thirty-five minutes, five seconds late. As a punishment: no dessert tonight." She didn't look at him to avoid watching those waters tremble.

"But, Alicia," he defended himself, "the traffic was very bad, there were a lot of people walking in the opposite direction, so many people that it was hard to walk two steps at a time. One had to carefully land on one foot, taking advantage of every little free spot, and keep the other foot in the air. This seems easy, I know it seems easy to you because you did not have to walk through that avenue this afternoon selling 'Wonder Soap: three bars for the price of one, they freshen up your life' but I assure you, it is a very difficult operation. Sometimes the foot suspended in the air got tired of being in that position. Remember, also, that a briefcase full of soap bars is very heavy. I tried to distract myself, to think about other things while I was holding my foot in the air, waiting for a small strip of blank sidewalk that I could use. One time I had a chance to finally put my foot on the ground but a man walking by me made an effort, moved his enormous square foot forward and reached the tile before I did."

"You should have moved him aside," the girl severely commented. Her father lowered his eyes. The soap briefcase was nearby; it was black. On its shiny leather a sign read: "Wonder Ltd. makes life more pleasant."

"It wouldn't have been easy," he defended himself. "That man was big, a stone lump; he was marching ahead decisively and quickly, ferociously propelled forward; he could have walked over me, smashing me as you smash an ant when you walk, inadvertently, with total indifference. That man and all the others were going somewhere, implacably, in a hurry." They had arrived in that country six months earlier but they had not found out yet the direction in which one was supposed to run. The father wasn't even sure that it was quite correct to run. "Where were they running?" asked Alicia with curiosity. "I don't know," he confessed. He tried furtively to light a cigarette, but she saw.

"Four," she brutally sentenced. "You have only one left."

"Three, I believe," he attempted to trick her. "If you remember, the one this morning I shared with you, and besides I couldn't enjoy it because I was in a hurry."

"Four," she repeated from her chair. Her blue dress and her long hair falling down her back made her resemble her mother. Her mother had never had a blue dress and always wore her hair short. According to the father those differences stressed the resemblance. Maybe the girl really looked like her mother's sister, but he wasn't quite sure. He had met her by coincidence at the supermarket; they had not been able to talk much because both were in a hurry. He had to feed the girl and write a paper on the influence of Edgar A. Poe on the poetry of a very famous writer nobody knew because he had never been out of his non-European country; she had to go immediately back to the hiding place of a guerrilla group for whom she was acting as a cover. She was a very nice young lady—he would never forget her red hair. It was surely a wig to better conceal her identity. He thought he would have liked enormously to show her his paper on the influence of Edgar A. Poe on the poetry of Raimundo Arias, even when she did not have time for those things; she looked at him with intelligence, intelligence devoured by passion, according to an expression of Raimundo Arias who, he was positive, had never met her yet he had intuited her.

She thought it was a pity that he was a bourgeois intellectual as her sister had said before abandoning him: he looked to be a tender and intelligent man.

In any case, he would never forget the red or blue or green or yellow hair of that young woman. "I should have gotten to know my wife's sister better," he reproached himself, but everybody was in a hurry: One had to make revolution, dinner, stand in line to buy bread, flour, rice, beans, oil, kerosene; one had also to run away from the assaults of the army, to take care of the little girl, product of a condom of the worst quality. Besides he was going to write a novel about the revolution; sometimes the novel got ahead of the revolution, sometimes the revolution ran so fast that it managed to get ahead of the novel, and meanwhile, his wife had left him—she surpassed both the revolution and the novel; the girl stayed with him. They had reached an agreement; it was not convenient to enter the guerrilla movement with a very small girl so, to hide the truth from everybody, he said that his wife had run away with another man, to Czechoslovakia.

"I should have gotten to know my sister's husband better," she had thought, but there wasn't enough time; she had to work, she had to stand in line to buy milk, bread, flour, rice, beans, oil, kerosene, she had to make revolution and, besides, sometimes she got sleepy.

"How many soap bars have you sold today?" asked Alicia, without moving from her seat in front of a small wooden table covered with colorful stones and a crystal giraffe. That was all that they had been able to rescue in their escape, when they had to leave their country because he had been accused of professing the Marxist-Leninist faith and of writing articles that were real anthems attempting to undermine the fatherland and the prestige of national institutions. Then, he had taken his daughter's hand with great dignity.

"I'm not an object to be carried in your arms," she had said. He had picked up a few papers, some clothes, and they had boarded the ship, under police control.

"Why don't we kill him now?" one military corporal had asked another. "We'll say, as always, that he died while trying to run away from the forces of order."

"Nobody is waiting for us," said the girl once they had arrived.

"Dear daughter," he had answered, "I'm not a soccer player." Alicia had looked at her father's extremely thin legs in the only pair of slacks that he owned. She thought as a daughter she was not very lucky. Her father wasn't a soccer player, nor was he a ship owner, nor a well known singer (The only song she had heard him sing was "A desalambrar*," and he was always out of tune; she sounded better singing the "Do tremble tyrants..." verse of the national anthem, which had been banned by the government because of its subversive character.) She wasn't very lucky indeed; her father was not the owner of a corporation, or a film star. Resignation. Children do not choose their parents but parents get to choose their children: "I'll take this one, Alicia; I won't take this one, abortion, no name."

"I've sold twenty-six, plus one that I gave an old lady, twenty-seven. The truth is that I didn't give it to the lady for nothing, she gave me three oranges in return. She was selling red healthy oranges, La Rioja oranges."

"Twenty six," the girl reflected, "not much for a whole day."

"You should be more considerate, my daughter. I believe that in this country people only take a bath on Sunday morning; besides, you must take the competition into account: gel, salts, powder soaps, cleaning lotions, soap flowers, solid foam and foam that solidifies." Not only was there no one waiting for them in that country—or in any other country—but in fact, the reception was rather hostile. As soon as they arrived the authorities requested an extraordinary amount of documents: father's ID, daughter's ID, father's passport, daughter's passport, father's visa, daughter's visa, father's certificate of no criminal record, daughter's certificate of no criminal record, certificate

---

*A very popular song about revolution of land reform

of baptism for both, certificate of being single ("How do you expect me to have it if I'm married?"). Well then, daughter's certificate of being single. . .and your marriage certificate. Father's certificate of elementary school, of high school, of higher education. Certificates of vaccinations against hepatitis, tetanus, tuberculosis, rabies, polio, meningitis, asthma, measles, chicken pox. The girl handed the certificates to the authorities, one by one, yellow and black certificates. Afterward, the girl neatly put them back in their places: Her father was very untidy. They also asked for the wife to be present so the girl could enter the country.

"That is not possible," said the father. "My wife has not come with us."

"Then the girl cannot enter," stated the immigration officer.

"Why?" the man asked. "I'm her father and I'll be responsible for her."

"Who says you are the father of this girl? Only her mother knows it."

"What about the papers?" the man asked. "Don't the papers say it, huh?"

"Papers are not proof of paternity," asserted the officer. "In fact only the mother can say if you are the real father of this kid."

"I'm not a kid, I'm a potential woman," said Alicia, outraged (she had learned that from her textbook).

"Her mother will have to come to reassure us that this girl is the fruit of her marriage to you," concluded the officer, threatening. "You might be a criminal, a kidnapper, a child rapist and this girl, your hostage."

"Ask her!" complained the father.

"This man is my father," confirmed the girl a few seconds later. To tell the truth, she had had the idea of denying it; it was the first time that to be his daughter, or not, depended on her, not on her parents. She could have said, for instance: "No, by no means is this man my father, he's an impostor," or something like that, as she had seen in soap operas. Then she could have chosen any father, or better, she could have become a sudden orphan, but she wasn't sure that solution was really the most adequate for her happiness. It was very hard to find a convenient father in your own country; abroad it could be even harder.

To become an orphan started to be interesting only past eighteen, when one was allowed into R-rated movies, when one could buy and sell without authorization and pay taxes. One could have children much earlier, at twelve or thirteen; it surely must be something less important because one could do that even before opening an individual savings account.

The authorities finally decided to do a blood test to prove his paternity. It wasn't that bad, after all. (Even though he fainted, as he did every time he saw blood. His wife used to say, "Revolution cannot be made this way!") It wasn't bad at all because they were taken to a very nice clinic. They were given a free meal after one more pint of blood than necessary was extracted from him as was usually done to foreigners, just because they were foreigners. She ate with great appetite.

"You're eating my blood," he said. He was so dizzy after the extraction that he could barely take advantage of his cafe au lait. She then ate two rations of bread and butter and apricot marmalade. They called peaches "apricots" in that country. In the country she came from, apricots were called "peaches." Newspapers never reported news from their country of origin; both the girl and her father found that in very poor taste.

"I would like to know what happened to the four hours they stole from me in the ship," she said after the test results confirmed that he, or any other fellow with a type A blood, was the kid's father.

After their fourth day on the ship, the captain's order had come through the sound system, reminding the passengers to turn watches thirty minutes ahead. At first the girl had resisted. She had kept her watch at 12:00 while everybody else on the ship was turning the hands around the dials, an activity that, in Alicia's opinion, showed an extreme frivolity in the treatment of time. Her father had not forced her to change the time. He was an anarchist and believed in freedom.

"Eat your berry ice cream, who knows when we'll be able to eat again," her father reminded her. Berries were strawberries, strawberries were berries in the country they had chosen because they already spoke the same language. "And bear in mind, daughter, that any individual rebelliousness is bound for failure," he had decreed while undauntedly looking at the girl's watch, which kept functioning at the measured rhythm of minutes and seconds. It was a very nice watch with a blue dial and silver numbers. Her mother had left it for her before leaving, surely because in the place she was heading to time was measured in different dimensions and life was more intense. Alicia, her eyes filled with tears, looked at the blue dial of her small watch (it looked like a lake, its hands like necks of two swans floating slowly). She had said:

"I will not turn it ahead for anything in the world." When they descended from the ship her watch was four hours behind.

"It's not that I'm behind, they are ahead," she said, looking at the two enormous clocks in the square. Finally, once she agreed (against her conscience) to adjust her watch to the time in that part of the world, she started to miss the four hours that had been stolen from her on the ship.

"What have they done to my five thousand, seven hundred and sixty minutes?" She asked her father. He wasn't ready with that answer. In fact he wasn't ready with any answer. He had been a son, also, for many years. He had lived as he had been able to live, which was good enough, and he was used to being robbed. He had had much more than four hours stolen from him, and he had not been able to do much to change the state of things. The state of things was determined by the owners of things, so every individual act of rebelliousness was bound for failure. . .With respect to his wife, wherever she was, if she was still anywhere, she had also been a daughter for many years, she had lived as she had been able to live, which was good enough, and she had devoted her life to changing the state of things, but things were resistant to change.

"Daughter, when we go back, they'll return those hours to you, if we ever go back. If we go back by ship."

That answer did not comfort her. She did not care for long-term returns. She felt completely humiliated, cheated. What would they do with so many stolen hours? She thought about ships loaded with stolen hours, silent ships that went through the ocean with their secret cargo of time. She thought about ghostly ships, about men guarding those areas where stolen time had been stored; she imagined hour-dealers waiting for the ships in dirty, dark ports, to buy hours and sell them afterwards. She thought of desperate men buying small boxes of insignificant time, poor victims of speculation. In a given port, an anxious man sees a ship arriving, a blue box is unloaded and he buys half an hour, maybe less than that, he buys ten minutes stolen from the unsuspecting passengers of a ship, robbed from involuntary emigrants, taken from the exiled. A desperate man is waiting at the port, looking at the big oil stains on the water, anxiously looking both ways, watching the white side of the arriving ship, the blue box, the insignificant time, that portion of time that for some reasons he needs and then the implacable voice of the Captain repeating: "Dear passengers, please be so kind as to turn your watches half an hour ahead," and it is no longer twelve, no longer twelve at night on board the white ship that moves with the rhythm of the waves. It is no longer the dark sea night at twelve. The passengers, impotent from so many lost battles, follow the orders docilely, adjust their watches and suddenly, it is no longer twelve but twelve-thirty. Thirty minutes have disappeared from their lives to fatten the storage areas of ships, to make time-dealers even wealthier.

"Damn those motherfucking ships," the girl desperately cried out.

Twenty-six soap bars was not a big deal, even when they only ate nuts and milk. "They have lots of calories," said her father, who knew about those things thanks to a workshop in parenting he had attended before Alicia's birth. He had learned about calories in food. He had learned the ten suitable answers a parent should produce when children start showing signs of sexual curiosity; he had learned how to clean and sterilize a bottle and what to do before the doctor arrived; but he had not learned a thing about surviving with children in a foreign country. He, therefore, kept silent contemplating the ceiling. It was a very ordinary ceiling, white, without significant geographical accidents. Alicia sighed, aware of her responsibilities. It was not a very nice job to have to be responsible for a father or a mother in those hard times. Even when her father was not very rebellious, he sometimes tried to make his own decisions and the enterprises he started from those decisions were almost sure to fail. Afterwards, she did not criticize him much because her father was very sensitive and she was afraid of discouraging him; it was necessary to stimulate his personal growth, even through those ill-fated initiatives. She had read a couple of manuals about adults and even when she did not completely agree with Freud (she preferred his rebellious disciple Lacan), she tried to avoid a worsening of her father's depressive neurosis. She was specially concerned for her father's sexual life; she thought it was too irregular and unstable. He could always find excuses to avoid discussing the subject. Sometimes he said he was too tired, other times, that he was not interested. When they walked the streets together and she made frequent comments on the women that passed by, he showed stubborn indifference. At first he alleged that he had to adapt his aesthetic standard, because the women there were very different from those in his country; later, he hinted something about the scarce use of soap; he finally praised the beauty of black women when everybody knew that in that country they had finished off the black people many, many years ago.

Alicia went to the box of French-made Chinese tea and checked its contents. There were a few coins left, all from different countries. They carried the portraits of various oppressors, almost none current. The bills were from the country they had left in the diaspora and no bank accepted them because they had no gold value whatsoever. She had thought of decorating the walls of that room with those blue bills but later she decided that it would have looked too folksy and she was a citizen of the world. Her father was not.

"We don't have any money," she said unemphatically. She said the same almost every day. Then her father looked into the pockets of his only suit. He found the address book with names of friends and acquaintances; he carefully checked it, without any results, because most of those people had died, no longer lived at those addresses or were thousands of miles away. However, he seemed to like that ritual. Friends almost always leave useless addresses behind.

"I don't think we have anybody to borrow from, today," her father commented, also unemphatically. Alicia sighed and went to the big hat box that she had stuffed with clothes before starting their trip.

"Wait, I'll be back in three or four hours," she told her father as she usually did while getting ready to leave. He then watched her with melancholy. She didn't look bad with that Indian costume he had given her for a school festivity. The feathers were somehow worn out and she had lost many on the trip. Alicia had painted them again, with watercolors, trying to give them an exotic, typical look. There were blue, red, yellow, black and white feathers.

"Do you have any idea of the kind of feathers the Charrua Indians sported?" she had asked her father. No way; the Spaniards had killed up to the last Indian in their country and there was a sole descendant alive, who claimed to be 104 years old, but he could be either Indian or Afghan. Her father wasn't even sure that the Indians wore feathers, as Metro Goldwyn Mayer liked to suggest. "Today I'm gonna add three more yellow ones, nobody will notice the difference," Alicia said.

She took her brushes and started to paint her face, trying to make very horrible grimaces. Tomato sauce was very good but she had once had a problem with a cat that had jumped on her, excited by the smell. Her father silently watched her, in admiration. Her skin was too clear to look like an Indian, but Europeans did not really care for details; not, at least, the kind of Europeans that were ready to stop in the street and give an Indian girl a few coins.

"Beware of the old men, my daughter, they are usually very libidinous," her father advised her every time she left. "Don't let any of them approach you; they are given to defloration..."

"Especially with virgin Indian girls," Alicia concluded, reciting the part of the speech she had already memorized.

She watched herself in the mirror. This time she had painted a horrifying grimace around her mouth. Some shadows around her eyes, the painted age line, the blue on her eyebrows and a fake scar gave her an air of antiquity she had seldom fabricated before. While looking at the mirror she said:

"I don't know whether to carry a sign that reads 'Latin American Indian Girl' or one with the words 'Elderly Latin American Indian Midget.'"

"I'm not sure that there were any midgets among the Indians," her father replied.

"Me neither," she said. That ignorance about their ancestors was a terrible thing. It was not the rule in Europe. People in Europe were better educated; they could always name five or six of their previous ancestors; they did not have revolutions and almost every country had a parliament, some with two chambers, some different.

Only once she had had a small accident while exhibiting herself in the Latin American Indian Girl costume. A terrible Machiavellian small boy, a little younger than she, had approached her and, with all his might, had pulled on her only Indian braid. In that moment she forgot that she should have uttered unintelligible sounds, and instead insulted him in perfect Spanish (which she did not hesitate to attribute to the fact that the Spanish had colonized the indigenous civilizations of the La Plata River). The incident had ended with Alicia's perfect strike to his jaw, which sent him and the Mother Country down to the ground.

Her father used to look at her in some anguish but with great admiration. He thought that something had changed in the genes from one generation to the other; obscured modification in their inherited characters had allowed current children to be perfect parents to their progenitors. It was a different race, furnished with unusual resistance; they had assimilated in their mother's wombs the lessons of the most intimate, the darkest of defeats. They had learned sadness, failure and desolation right from their mother's uterus. Later, when they saw light, they already knew how to live despite everything. Conceived in bitter nights, in nights of persecution, uncertainty, misery and terror, conceived in houses that looked like jail cells or in jail cells that were tombs, in beds fit for coffins, the survivors of those nights of torture and pain were born under the sign of resistance and endurance.

Alicia looked at him before leaving. Her head was crowned with feathers and her straw skirt covered in part her very white legs. Her torso was nude, her incipient, discretely round breasts ending in tender soft pink nipples. She did not carry an arrow because her father could never buy her one; he was always short of money. Their eyes met, different, but transparent. They both knew how to decipher the codes of eyes. They had learned to do it at sea, during those long nights of insomnia, when not even the moon was shining.

There, while smoking rationed cigarettes and plotting ways of grabbing a ham sandwich from the kitchen, they had learned to read the waters of eyes, quiet waters of the father, restless waters of the daughter's lake. Alicia looked at him and read; she read the mystification, the dreams, the sadness. So when she opened the door and disguised her voice to go along with her Latin-American-Indian-girl-lost-in-Europe costume, she told him clearly: "I'm positive that what you think about my generation is completely wrong."

Translated by Alicia Partnoy and Regina M. Kreger

Marta Traba
Argentina

Born in 1930, Marta Traba lived in France, Colombia, Uruguay and the United States. She won the 1966 Casa de las Américas prize and authored thirty-three volumes of fiction, poetry, essays and art criticism. She founded the Museum of Modern Art in Colombia, the country from which she was expelled by the government due to political reasons. In 1979, she came to the United States as a professor, but she had to leave in 1983, again for political reasons—the INS denied her a visa. She died in a plane crash that very same year. Marta Traba left an unpublished novel that was later printed in Mexico, En cualquier lugar (In Any Place), *from which this fragment has been excerpted.*

The Day Flora Died

She used to close her eyes and envision the green house full of
carnations. It was difficult at first, because she had never seen
them before, but at last she was able to imagine them with that rare
precision she had for everything that was insignificant. There they
were, one in front of the other, their ruffled edges fresh, their petals
protruding from a green bulb that made you want to grind it with
your teeth. The image repeated itself regularly, even though she knew
all too well that everything was a lie. Or maybe because of this,
because it was all a lie, she guarded it more, having lost all notion of
truth and falsehood. She had asked herself when and how it began
until she was worn out, and at last she had to let that go too.

But there were many sleepless nights when she crept from her
room and saw in the distance a round window and a big ball ever
glowing, day and night, or the figure of a tree changing from green to
a ghostly white, a phantasm. Then her thoughts wandered; it was
autumn again and her hands shook in a way that made it necessary to
grasp the ledge of the window with all her strength. But in the
morning who could have imagined such torment?

With surprising care, she selected each blouse to match each
skirt and jacket. She brushed, forty times, twenty times on each side,
her straight black hair—hair that had become shorter as the years
passed, but which still hung over her left cheek to be tossed back with

a defiant motion of the head. She quickly walked down the steps of the building and walked next to the curb. As she raised her hand to flag a taxi, an abrupt pain overwhelmed her. Where was she? In what city? Where was she going? She came out of the sudden confusion determined to recognize her daily route. And then the name of the city began to spell itself out and the feeling of imminent danger started to subside.

This was how it was. With every turn, the world became more a place of unknown syllables forming strange words. It was impossible to rebuild a single phrase. Each word was a plank floating on a rough, silent sea without a shore, and there she was holding on. She looked at the sad state of her broken nails. Had this storm destroyed them? She laughed softly. The taxi turned alongside the truck loaded with the hanging T-shirts. Yes, the name of the city was reassuringly written there, in all sizes. What would happen if she were to see another name printed there one day? She refused to consider it. The taxi pulled up to the sidewalk and stopped in front of the stairs. She got out and looked to the top of the stairs. While the taxi driver put the fare in his pocket, he told her have a nice day. He also looked up, but when he saw the same old statue as always he shrugged his shoulders and pulled away. The statue grew in size as she drew near, and certain ridiculous details became apparent. For example, the sculptor has placed the buttonholes on the wrong side of this illustrious man's vest. His face was unimpressive, even foolish, yet the two frowns that creased his forehead caused you to think. But he was a mystery and she preferred it that way. Filled with inexplicable scorn, she bypassed the inscription on the statue's front and condemned the man to oblivion. Almost immediately, she opened the large doors, walked mechanically to her desk and reviewed the never-ending pile of index cards.

Not much time passed before the telephone rang. Luis. She reconciled herself with the thought as she lifted the receiver. She knew it was him and she knew what he would say — Lucho, something's up — she knew all the details but feigned ignorance as if it were life that could be found in these little retaliations.

"Hello," Luis said. "Who's this?" She knew he wouldn't let on

118

because he, too, was staking his life.

"Lucho," he said, his voice barely audible. "Something's up." She had the craziest desire to laugh, but she withheld it. One day, who could tell when, there really would be something new.

"Can you hear me?" he whispered. Barely; if you talked a bit louder I'd hear better. "No, I can't." She imagined more than she understood.

"Things have become pretty ugly."

"Oh, do you mean good for us?" she asked in a soft murmur.

"It depends how you look at things."

With a flash of impatience, she insisted, "I'd like to know how you look at things."

"Right now, everything's peachy. But Pablo still has to decide."

"Pablo who?" she asked, knowing that nothing could make him angrier. But he wasn't in the mood for her games.

"We already spoke to Raul and he agrees with everything. We're going to have to put up a fight tonight."

She was about to ask against whom, but soon realized the foolishness of their little game. She remained silent, held the phone over her shoulder, and fingered the index cards. This, of course, was just what he wanted. Now the conversation was his, no idiotic interruptions.

"We discovered, just like we suspected, that the person who arrived in the cafe the night before last couldn't be trusted." Pause. "Raul set the trap and he fell for it like a fish takes to water. We have four heavy-duty contradictions in our war chest." Pause. "This means they're going to be in a tight spot tonight and the group is liquidated." Pause. The silence was uncomfortable and he asked, "Are you listening to me?"

"Yeah," she replied unwillingly. "Now what?"

"I can't tell you over the phone. Aren't you going to drop by the station today?"

"I'm not going to wait for anybody," she finally responded. "It's demoralizing for me to see all those people jammed together. It reminds me of the crowds standing in front of the posted new releases during the war." A small laugh was heard on the other side of the line.

"The 1914 war?"

"No," she said, "the English invasions."

She gave the card she had in her hand a perplexed look. She asked, since he was already on the phone, if so and so had died.

"December 3, 1978," Luis said. He had a monster of a memory. She mentioned it to him and laughed. "Your memory wears out when you reach thirty—one more year to go before I become like you."

"And I have to go back twenty to get it back," she replied too quickly. It had embarrassed her to take five years off her age.

But he didn't retreat. "Come on, beautiful, let's not take off too many years."

Then she felt enraged and cursed herself for wasting time with such an imbecile. She tried to hide her irritation and calmly asked why he had called. Didn't he have anything better to do in this bitch of a life?

Millions of things, he said, he couldn't spare a minute more.

"In that case, *smetela*," she said in her best Italian, and hung up. She immediately regretted losing control and thought she'd never learn how to handle Luis. Not Luis, or anybody, for that matter. And then the sharp pain in her left temple pulsing again. It was nothing, she wouldn't accept the alibi. Even if she were in pieces, she had to go and see Flora, give a long explanation, perhaps even ask forgiveness—do something monstrous and out of proportion, like kneeling before her, and Flora, horrified, would reject it. She had to do something abnormal and uncalled for, and that would reflect the extent of her shock and her true and terrible penance. She shuffled through the index cards with the speed of a madwoman. A while later the telephone rang again. She didn't want to answer, but it rang until she had no other option. Oh, God. Could it possibly be Luis again? She didn't have time to enter the Luis-Lucho game.

"This time she hit the mark," he said and there was an immense pause. "Flora, in the heart." He hung up.

She remained completely frozen, her two hands grasping the top of the desk. A while later she placed one hand over the other and it felt cold and distant. She thought, "Perhaps I, too, am dead." The relief was indescribable.

Translated by Andrea Vincent

III.

The Torch That Sheds My Light: Essay

Marta Benavides
El Salvador

*Born and raised in El Salvador, Marta Benavides
worked as a student organizing migrant farmworkers
in Southern New Jersey. She is an educator, sociolo-
gist, theologian and an ordained Baptist minister. She
directed the Ecumenical Committee for Humanitarian Aid (CEAH) under the sponsorship of Archbishop Oscar Romero. The committee created the
first refugee centers in El Salvador. Marta Benavides
coordinates Ecumenical Ministries for Development
& Peace (MEDEPAZ), which works with Salvadorans in Mexico, Central America, United States and El
Salvador. In her own words, her greatest desire is to
be back to live, work and die in El Salvador.*

El Salvador: The Presence Removed

O ne more half decade to make five hundred years. That is 1992. Five hundred years since he left for the Indies in search of spices and got lost. Yet, he claimed to have discovered us. He called us Indians, and the islands of the eastern Caribbean, the West Indies.

It was an encounter; it could have been good. But the Spanish took possession of the lands and the people; our women were raped, our culture destroyed, our records burned. We were neither Christian nor Western. The Spanish thought we had no civilization. The *"encomenderos"* were to guide our souls to salvation. That is what that name was all about. They chained our people and forced them to work. Slavery, captivity, just like the Jews in Babylon.

The National Autonomous University of El Salvador was closed in June 1980; the books were burned, the campus completely ransacked, the leaders, who were students, professors and workers, killed, jailed or banished. It was just like the times of the Spanish conquest. Thinking and knowing are still considered dangerous today. As an example, the International Monetary Fund recommends cuts in the curriculum. No history, ethics or art. That should wait until more prosperous times. Technical skills should be taught in order to produce more, export more, and pay our international debt.

Webster's dictionary defines an exile as "one banished, to

wander aimlessly, roam; a prolonged living away from one's country, community, usually enforced, banishment; prolonged separation from one's country or home as by stress or circumstances. Expulsion from one's native land by authoritative decree. Expatriate. *The exile*: the Babylonian captivity of the Jews in the 6th century B.C." — a *very* good definition, clear and complete. It is the reality, the experience of the expatriate. It is also the reality for the *patria*, the motherland.

I became aware of the term *exile* at a very young age. Coming from a Latin American country, which had been under the military one way or another for the last fifty years, I grew up knowing about coups d'etat. Each time our nation went through such an experience, some people would lose their jobs. Then a new provisional government would be formed. Sometimes it would be a military junta. Only one or two reform-minded civil-military coalitions have existed in the last thirty years. There would always be satire and political jokes about the ones who were ousted. Soon after, the jokes would be about the new government as well. It was the way the people would be able to express their opinions and discontent. On the days following the coup, the details, embellished by popular creativity, would be widely known.

During one of the coups, the military went in the middle of the night and picked up people in their night clothes. The people were not even given the chance to change. They were taken to the airport and sent, most of the time, in an army airplane out of the country: to Costa Rica, Nicaragua, Guatemala or Mexico. One ex-president and his family was said to have lost everything they had been able to acquire before and during their tenure. This particular president was known for his extremely repressive regime marked by anti-labor practices and unpopular law. The story goes that the family started a shack to sell *pupusas* (a typical food eaten by the poor people of El Salvador) in San Jose, Costa Rica. The wife, who was so elegant and classy, who used to hold prestigious get-togethers at the presidential palace in San Salvador. . . She was the leader of the wives of the government association; they, who wore new dresses as they poured a cup of milk for poor children at La Vega once a month. Well, no more. Poor woman. She and her daughters had to serve the *pupusas* in San Jose.

124

There is another story. This is the case of the chief of the national police. The colonel was sent into so-called political exile, as military attache to the Salvadoran embassy to the Somoza dynasty dictatorship in Nicaragua. He happened to have been caught stealing too much, too quickly, too openly before he was able to develop a good base for himself among his peers. His greed, and the envy of the others, got him. The poor man the colonel hired as a policeman was robbed of two to three months salary, the family's chickens and the eggs, the sugar and the cow. This colonel also robbed the well-to-do, whenever he could. They lost houses in upper-class communities, their orange groves in beautiful Los Planes, the *rancho* at the secluded seashore. Once he stole a whole small island at the Espiritu Santo Bay — cattle, crops, huts and the people with it! The exile proved to be a good school for this family. Both parents and children became more efficient at exploitation and practicing racism and classism.

In the last ten years, the youngest son, the major, rose up through the ranks of the army and the repressive machinery. He climbed to the post of director of the school for the famously repressive National Guard. One of his closest associates was the head honcho of the Salvadoran death squads, or "squash" as our people refer to them. In the early eighties, the major went into "exile." The head of the death squads also did, as the result of having been captured plotting a coup against Duarte while at the coffee plantation in Santa Tecla, on the outskirts of San Salvador. The newspapers reported that some of those captured tried to eat some of their documents. Information was found on them that referred to attempts to overthrow the government, and to plots to murder people like Monsignor Romero. The two men and others were detained and put in jail for a few days. However, before they appeared in court, threats to the judge and other members of the judicial system "forced" the government to dismiss the case for lack of evidence. They went into "voluntary exile" in Guatemala. From that neighboring country, they continued to plot, broadcast TV programs. Anything that was different was attacked as communist. Many kinds of threats were made.

Many of the Salvadoran oligarchy also moved to Guatemala,

unable to live in peace, they said, in our country. Some others moved to Miami. The major and his friend moved back and forth between Guatemala, Miami and El Salvador. They all said they were in "exile." One has to see the magnificent homes just outside Guatemala City on the way to El Salvador to have an idea of how splendid and glamorous exile can be! In two years, these men were back in El Salvador, legitimized as leaders of "opposition" political parties, with much money and support from very conservative forces, including U.S. senators. As a result of the U.S.-sponsored election, they were able to form a political coalition of the right and ultra-right. They became the majority in the legislature; the well-known leader of the death squads became the president. This quite effectively tied the small reforms sponsored by the U.S. government to the Christian Democrat president of El Salvador.

The people in the real opposition, who were the trade unionists, the teachers, the peasants, the members of political parties, the women of the markets, the peoples of the marginalized communities and the students, did not experience the same type of life. No, they were picked up in the streets, tortured and disappeared. They were machine gunned on street corners. Very, very seldom did they make it to jail. A few of them were able to escape and run away to Guatemala, for a few months or a year or two. Only a few, like Mr. Duarte and Mr. Ungo, were put on a plane for Venezuela. Mr. Duarte was elected president of El Salvador, having chosen to cooperate with the plan for "modernization" and "reform" as envisioned and sponsored by the United States. Mr. Ungo lived in "voluntary exile" in Panama. He was considered a terrorist, and would have been captured upon return to El Salvador. He is currently president of the Democratic Revolutionary Front, a broad opposition coalition in alliance with the Farabundo Martí National Liberation Front (FMLN). The FMLN is the coalition of the five popular military groups which seek peace and justice through dialogue and negotiation. This alliance was actively involved in bringing about the process of the Central American Peace Pact signed by the five Central American presidents on August 7, 1987.

The political, social and economic situation is constantly becoming more critical. The people grow stronger in their demands for equality and justice. The economic conditions of the country worsen with the world crisis. The two percent of the population who own half of the country need to maintain law and order. They are "good businessmen and capitalists," and they know that profits must increase. On the other hand, the military has become better trained and equipped to do a good job at maintaining "business as usual."

The people have been organizing for years. They have no money but much wisdom and a strong will to win. They won the presidential elections in 1972...Ungo and Duarte, and a few others, were banished; thousands were repressed as they denounced fraud; dozens were killed, disappeared or jailed, but they don't look back except to learn. They are determined to continue to move forward, grabbing and creating the future as always. The National Unity for Opposition (UNO), the people's organization, again wins the presidential election. The story of repression is repeated, only this time it is much worse. The candidates and their closest aides are exiled. It's 1977, and the popular league, 28th of February, is born. This represents one more step in the struggle...fewer people believe that the vote will bring the change for democracy representative of the needs and aspirations of the nation. The military governments start to tremble, and the military represses without a mask. The ultra-right, hiding in the shadows, puts posters on telephone poles: "Be a patriot, kill a Jesuit." Soon it's: "Be a patriot, kill a priest."

In just a few more weeks, mimeographed leaflets, containing threats of death to those involved in the people's movement, are thrown to people as they wait at bus stops. The distributors are armed men in sunglasses, in Cherokees with polarized glass windows...*Sopilotes*, scavenger birds, eat the remains of mutilated human bodies thrown out each night at El Playon, a beach close to the capital.

More than a quarter of a million people are marching on the streets demanding better salaries and jobs, a stop to the repression, a stop to the persecution and killing of the priests, freedom for the political prisoners, and no more disappearances...January 22, 1980, the people march united under the banner of the Revolutionary

Coordinator of the Masses of the People, in memory of the fallen of the January 22nd insurrection of 1932. (Thirty thousand were killed by the military in the two weeks of the insurrection under the guise of saving El Salvador from communism. We know this as *La Matanza*—The Big Slaughter. The people remember, the dead will never be forgotten. In downtown San Salvador, people were shot from the top of government buildings, banks and the coffee growers association headquarters. Many people were killed, disappeared, and jailed.) Each popular organization has provided security for the march. For the first time in our history they march prepared to respond to gunfire if necessary. While some of the security forces rescue the masses from the gunfire, the others respond to the snipers.

We are Salvadoran and we love our country. The rich and the military, in alliance with multinational corporations, have tried to banish us, to prevent us from claiming our right to own our land and forge a future as a nation. As far as they are concerned, we are to work, and to live for work. This is a modern-day equivalent of slavery. No decisions are ours, and we mustn't try to change our situation, for we are in exile, and in captivity in our own land.

I am working with Monsignor Romero, Archbishop of San Salvador. We sponsor the National Ecumenical Committee for Humanitarian Aid. Our commitment is to respond to the needs of all the people hurt by the violence, to walk with our people in the process of reclaiming our land. No more captivity; we must free ourselves from the coffee, cotton and sugar barons. We must redirect and rebuild a land of milk and honey for all, for this is the measure of true development. Monse, as I call him, calls everyone to unite in the efforts to bring peace with justice and dignity, not the peace of the cemeteries! "Stop the violence," he cries. He asks the rich to give up their expensive rings and other jewelry, before the poor take it from them. The hungry must be fed. From the soldiers, he demands that they not obey the officer's call to kill the brother. He asks the popular organizations to work in unity for a common program to benefit the masses. He asks the people for discipline and unity, and to demand political accountability from the organizations.

The marches are repressed, the strikes militarized, the union people hunted, jailed, tortured. Again thousands are killed including priests, nuns and catechists. Monsignor Romero... executed as he serves communion in church. The president and executive board of the Democratic Revolutionary Front (FDR) are kidnapped, tortured, and murdered during the United States' Thanksgiving weekend of 1980. Just a week later, as we are ready to hold the funeral for these brothers, the four religious women from the United States suffer the same luck; they are also raped.

You, who work in humanitarian aid, be sure not to aid the enemy. Not with one cup of water. Not even a child is exempt. Ah! But you work with the Salvadoran Red Cross? Oh yes, that is a prestigious, respectable board made up of the most successful Salvadoran businessmen. Yes, the Red Cross is legitimate; it abides by the rules. It only helps when the government calls, aiding in emergencies and catastrophes. It's the Green Cross which is the problem, since people from the barriadas, the ghettos, and La Fosa are active in it. They are, to say the least, possible subversives, I mean, leftist sympathizers.

And me, ah...I am directing the National Ecumenical Humanitarian Aid. No, the refugee centers which we had to set up are not leftist nests. It's just that hundreds of old people and women and children had to leave the rural areas because of the militarization imposed for the agrarian reform. Many have been forced to wander in the mountains and are caught in the crossfire. They are not hiding anything. It's just that they watched as some of their relatives were killed by members of the military. Other relatives were captured and never seen again. So they did not want to take refuge in the army barracks, schools or Red Cross tents as you requested from your loudspeakers. They wanted Monsignor Romero's help. No, I don't believe they are hiding any crimes against the government, nor are they subversive terrorists...what do you mean that if we help them we must be as subversive as they are? No, it's not because I want to politicize the issue that I refer to them as refugees.

This is a mere fact: they are looking for refuge; they are homeless. Yes, you are right, our committee did not accept the U.S. Embassy's donation for disaster relief to buy mattresses for the refugees. It was not at all that we wanted more money or that it was too little, for it was thousands of dollars. We sent a letter thanking President Jimmy Carter, and asked him to heed the call of Monsignor Romero to stop giving any more aid to the Salvadoran military. That is the only help we want and need.

Oh, I am hiding. I must continue to do everything underground. They came after me. They're hunting me down...just like most of my friends...can't go to their funerals; we only help to bury them, to support their wives and children left behind...I can't see you either, Ita*, no more working together. I hug you goodbye. The repression continues, but after October 1980, the mountains and cities tremble.

Human rights violations are decreasing in El Salvador. From an average of more than two hundred murders a week, we're down to thirty, the State Department says. *The disappeared? They just left and didn't let their families know. Well, a few probably were the victims of Mano Blanca* (one of many death squads), *but that is subsiding you see, and that is what counts. The death squads are under control and the ultra-right executions have stopped. Everyone must participate in the democratic process and participate in elections. The ultra-right is becoming civilized, is understanding that it must form its political parties. The U.S. Embassy has been applying pressure at the right places. As you know, the United States will only send aid if Duarte or one like him gets elected. No, no, no, the million displaced people are the result of the civil disorder and strife caused by the Marxist guerrillas supported by the international terrorists of Nicaragua, Cuba, Russia, and Libya. They are not uprooted, neither exiles nor political refugees. That's the reason that no asylum is granted to them, unless they can prove beyond a doubt that their lives are in danger for political reasons. So, in the United States they are arrested and kept in detention at Corralon and other similar centers. They have left El Salvador voluntarily. All those who left for other countries, and especially*

---

*Ita Ford, one of the murdered sisters.

for the United States, are nothing but economic refugees.

The snow is so deep. There is a Salvadoran family clinging together. They talk with a Chilean accent now, for Chileans have helped to make the arrangements to unite this family and continue to provide support. They are making tortillas at five in the morning before they go to work. There is a heavy winter storm in the small town of Medicine Hat, Canada. They stand behind the glass of the front door, and we keep looking at each other, our hands waving goodbye until I can't see them any longer because the car makes a turn.

No, there are no exiles. El Salvador has not exiled citizens for a while now. They all leave voluntarily. . . One sells everything one has to buy the ticket and the visa to go to Mexico. No roots — no anything. Except the desire to be back. We have to make it back some day. We are making that day.

I'm sorry, no, I'm not in voluntary exile. No, I hate it. I have been forced out. My country has been taken from me, and I'm not a tourist, even though I have a tourist visa. Mexico can't take a position on our situation. It would terribly hinder Mexico's work for peace in Central American through the Contadora initiative. Mexico would be accused of taking sides with the left of El Salvador if it granted us political asylum. Mexico has helped us so much, and the people have been like our own. But this is a different historical moment. We had to flee our country. It's not at all like the support provided to the brothers and sisters who had to leave Chile because of the coup of September 1973.

Voluntary exile. What a contradiction! What an irony! None of us wants to be anywhere but home. Who would voluntarily choose to be banished and estranged from home? There is a gathering of people in the United States who work with Central American refugees. I am the only one in exile. I sit and listen: "It's fascinating and exciting."

"Very interesting. . ." someone says, "What are your plans?"

"Well, I'm thinking of spending six months in Central America, I need a change. I'll probably go at the beginning of 1988."

"Oh, wow, what will you do, where will you go? Will you visit various countries in the region as you did before?"

"Well, no, I am not sure. . . I think I need to replenish myself, but I need to get out of the States. Salvador is nice, but I don't like it. Too much noise there! I don't know how people can take it there; the loud speakers with the protest songs, all the political agitation, so much trash around, and such poverty! No, I guess I'll go to Guatemala this time. Yeah, I hear Guatemala is great, and the Spanish courses are much cheaper. It's one-to-one, such flexibility . . .weekends are off to do whatever you want. Maybe go over to El Salvador and check it out."

Oh, God, my country, my people. Let me hold them close to my heart, let me love them. This dirty wretched little country of mine, let me bathe it and powder it just like Roque* said.

. . .Go away, let us stay home. I am barred, barred from living in my land in these historic moments. Foreigners come and go, they visit our prisoners, buy food that they don't eat; they are too much in a hurry to learn about us, but they don't know us. They can pay respect to our dead while we hide in the shadows, in the crowds, keeping our faces from being seen. Someone else writes about our sorrows, someone else sings about our pain, for even the Salvadorans who write our theology have been born and raised someplace else.

> By the rivers of Babylon we sat down and wept
> when we remembered Zion.
> There on the willow-trees
> we hung up our harps,
> for there those who carried us off
> demanded music and singing,
> and our captors called on us to be merry:
> 'Sing us one of the songs of Zion.'
> How could we sing the Lord's song
> in a foreign land?

---

*Roque Dalton, famous poet of El Salvador, died in 1975.

If I forget you, O Jerusalem,
   let my right hand wither away;
let my tongue cling to the roof of my mouth
   if I do not remember you,
if I do not set Jerusalem
   above my highest joy.
Remember, O Lord, against the people of Edom
   the day of Jerusalem's fall,
when they said, 'Down with it, down with it,
   down to its very foundations!'
O Babylon, Babylon the destroyer,
   happy the man who repays you
   for all that you did to us!
Happy is he who shall seize your children
   and dash them against the rock.

— Psalm 137 New English Bible

We can't sing the joyous songs. Yet we sing. We sing about our pain, or to teach self-defense and revolutionary principles. We sing to make fun of Duarte and the U.S government, and we sing the songs of the future, of peace with justice which we, the Salvadorans, are daring to grab, even by force, from the hands that murder us. We will be home!

Gracias mil a mis compañeras Judy y Meredith por su ayuda.

133

Griselda Gambaro
Argentina

Griselda Gambaro is one of the few Latin American women playwrights. She lived in exile during the time of the military rule in Argentina. Her works have been performed worldwide, and a collection of her plays will soon be published in the United States. Griselda Gambaro has also written several novels. She selected the following excerpt from Dios no nos quiere contentos *(God Does Not Want Us Happy).*

The Talks That Never Took Place

The circus is the present, Tristan, and a deception of the past. When I approach the Big Boss, there is no point in asking questions. He is quick to humiliate — it's his circus. Those who make it move, those who create the show, have no say in it at all. The possession of the tent is more important than the tent itself and all that happens beneath it.

I don't get older, Tristan. In spite of my thinning and dyed hair, with my wrinkles and all, I'm still the same person. I can coil and uncoil at ease; I can jump from one trapeze to the other with a lightness that defies gravity. What really makes me older is silence, the kind of silence when nothing can be named.

When I hear the commands of the Big Boss, the clapping, or the clown's voice guiding the audience to their seats, when the clown screams his emaciated jokes on stage, transforming that cruelty he endures into laughter, when I hear all that, I hear only silence.

I'm no longer accustomed to the spoken word. My gestures deteriorate, because they only can grow in weight and meaning when they can be complemented by the words and the gestures of others. But nobody speaks amidst this strained silence, nobody names his or her actions or the actions of others, because to name means to discover, to uncover. Neither voices nor screams can penetrate that wrapping of cotton and plaster that envelops us as if we were asleep in a big house.

It's as if a barbaric and painful disgrace coats everything, a disgrace born of confusion, of the weakness of many and the power of few. Only if the crime is called by its name, and we recognize it by name, can even a petty retribution be possible. Only then can crime be conquered by justice. But justice no longer exists. The circus is pure falsehood and sometimes, when I'm up there, it seems to me that I don't shed light on anybody. That not even the respite of jumping from one trapeze to another will be granted to me if that silence continues.

* * *

There are days when I tell myself everything is fine. The death of those we loved will correspond in time with our own death and will make it acceptable, and what we cannot understand at the height of our desperation will be revealed to us at some point.

When I'm up there, creature of ambiguity, yet not ambiguous myself, I know everything is fine, Tristan. I'm swinging up there, and I know that everything is fine, even though I'll never understand the reasonability or arbitrariness of disgrace. I don't know an answer other than that one. I advise myself as I would advise someone who is hurt and begs for a word: I tell myself this is a good answer, it should be enough. I grab onto it as to the trapeze crossbars and I shift in the air, and from the chaos of movement, I choose those movements that I can organize with that answer that is no answer. I transform myself, I choose that answer as true and mine and it is more genuine and mine than any other answer that is hidden from me by an indifferent Wisdom. Up on the trapeze—but on Earth, I have the right to severely question my fate, so any fate can be mine except for that of being a child of bitterness. That is why I do cry, Tristan. Everything is fine.

Translated by Alicia Partnoy

Isabel Morel Letelier
Chile

Isabel Letelier is a sculptor and human rights activist. She came to the United States a year after the 1973 coup in Chile. Her husband, Orlando Letelier, was killed in Washington D.C. by the Chilean secret police. Isabel is the director of the Human Rights Project and the Third World Women's Project at the Institute for Policy Studies in Washington D.C. She travels extensively, speaking on human rights, Third World women's rights and the role of the Church in present Chilean society.

Introduction to Chile

You are hard, my Chile, as a bone
lean and naked, my Chile.
The sun overhead bites you,
the sea like a blue cow licks you;
lapping your wounds,
the ragged shore.

The waves piercing your side
lick you with universal sea.

—*Juvencio Valle,*
Mi Chile Horizontal Del Monte
en La Ladera (1960)

My house was very large, with many rooms, flowers, and birds. In vain, my brothers, my sister and I would try with our voices to arouse all of its sleepy corners. Yet the silence always remained hidden in some corridor.

In the mornings a sweet patient teacher would come to teach us to read. It would be difficult to find us. We grew up among the trees in the orchard. We would build cities of mud between the henhouse and the canal, or for hours we would contemplate the snails making love between the violets.

One day, due only to the stubbornness of my teacher, I found myself reading without pause the last page of the primer. There, awaiting me as if it were a prize for my efforts, was a reading of mountains and sea, entitled "My Country." From then on, reading for me became a dazzling game that had me devouring for years my parents' library, along with the oranges from the garden.

But as the days passed and my readings advanced, that blue and white country I had discovered at the end of my reading book became filled with people who were suffering. Gabriela Mistral, in her verses and serenades, brought closer to us the pain of the humble children, of the countryside, of the city and of the desert.

During our adolescence, Pablo Neruda showed us the sensual texture of love; later with his magic tongue, he made the stone of Machu Picchu, the simple onions, the bloodied streets of Spain, and the liberating song of our land speak to us.

But not all were able to comprehend the message of the poets and writers. In his "Intimacy Speech" of 1970, Pablo Neruda said, "First: no more illiterates. We don't want to continue being writers of people who don't know how to read. We don't want to feel shame, the ignorance of a static and leprous past. We want more books, more magazines, more culture."

For one thousand days, the popular government of Salvador Allende worked to give bread, shelter, clothing, and culture to the people. Through its poets, writers and artists the popular spirit of Chile produced a genuine explosion of culture. The arts became interwoven and artists joined hands in a common labor. The popular musicians sang to the poets and the muralists painted to the writers. And so, the brilliant star of our culture shone with promise for those who, for the first time, began to enjoy her.

But one day in September 1973, machine guns, hate and fire killed people, burned books and shattered the star into a thousand pieces, scattering them among the streets of the world. Some of the fragments remained to sow and fertilize our land. These writers today are not permitted to publish their works, but they and their readers, in an act of love and danger, search and find innovative forms of dialogue. And so, printed manuscripts are passed from hand to hand uniting people and hopes.

The dictatorship attempts to submerge the literature in silence; but if in any other part of the world the occupation of writer is considered a personal office, in Chile, as in the rest of Latin America, it bears a social responsibility. The themes of our literature must speak to the harsh economic reality and the social degradation imposed upon the majority by a small group in power. Nor can there be absent from them the fundamental necessity of liberating action.

There are, of course, writers on our continent whose only theme is the concentric chaos of their own lives. While their discourse does not reflect any pressing reality, maintaining themselves by speculating among the celestial spheres, the regime publishes their books, bestows them with smiles and medals, and presents them before the national public as the positive soul of the fatherland. Fortunately, this kind of writer does not abound in our land. Then there are a few others that write directly for the dictatorships, but they, as Julio Cortázar says, "are not writers; they are nothing more than court clerks."

The writer that lives under repression knows that each of his sentences occupies a space of imposed silence. He collects the multiplicity of gestures that oppose the dictatorship and he writes a book that is transformed into a manifesto, with each of the readers subscribing in silence.

I have said that the dialogue established between writer and reader in Chile is filled with love and risk. Risk because repression and jail can result with the turn of any page; love because the need for fulfillment must be greater than in any other situation.

But what happens to the writer who is expelled from the country? The first readers of this writer's work are easy to identify. They are every one of the one million Chileans who live in exile. These readers are easy to reach because of their need to see themselves as a continuation of their past. These Chileans are characterized by their stubborn cultural dedication to the artistic development achieved with whole popular participation in Chile under the government of Salvador Allende.

During the last few years I have visited the homes of my compatriots in the most diverse cites of the world and I have seen how the cultural reviews and the books of Chilean writers occupy such important places in the little libraries in these homes. The desire to maintain one's culture, despite the difficulties of the surrounding conditions, extends to all the cultural ambits. So, for example, in every country where there are Chileans, we see musical folk groups, theater groups, *peñas* or mural brigades which bear witness to the essence of who we are.

But the writer in exile has another reader, one more coveted but with whom the dialogue is made very difficult by the distance the dictatorship imposes. That reader lives in Chile. With the hope of re-establishing communion with him, Chilean writers form cultural journals, like *Araucaria*, edited by Volodia Teitelboim or *Literatura en Exilio*, edited by Fernando Alegría and David Valjalo. Forums of Chilean culture are held, like the one in Poland in May of 1980, initiated by the President of the Polish Chile Solidarity Committee, Edmund Osmanczyk. There, in the city of Torun, where in another time Copernicus detained the sun and put our earth into movement, writers and artists from Chile met with intellectuals from other parts of the world for the common task of defending with concrete action the Chilean culture.

Julio Cortázar, a participant in the event, posed the question, "What can we do from here, from the countries of Europe, to stimulate the advance of culture in Chile? In what measure and in what form can we help so that poetry is ever more and more in the streets. . . Imagine a publishing house that afforded the best of the innumerable manuscripts that circulate within and outside of Chile and whose contents are often a splendid weapon of combat. . . I imagine the creation of a fund to benefit the work of the Chilean fine artists in exile and to bring from Chile others who cannot develop their art and, above all, make it known inside the country. . . If some of this materializes as a result of this meeting, we won't have come to it in vain; if, above and beyond the words, are born efficacious accomplishments, we shall all regard this encounter as an enormous step forward."

Now, in the same spirit, in New York, the PEN American Center and its Freedom to Write Committee have taken the initiative to publish a book of essays about the culture of Chile. What does it mean to be a writer in a country where the government is a military dictatorship that annihilates all forms of opposition? I leave you with the voice of a young poet of the Generation of '73 who sings to us from the depths of our native land:

Though the days may pass
And other galaxies exist
In order to die
We await your return
It will never be late
The hurt of the country
Is a song no one sings
But to which all listen.

Translated by Nena Terrell

Clara Nieto de Ponce de León
Colombia

Clara Nieto de Ponce de León is a journalist and career diplomat who served in the Colombian delegation to the United States from 1957 to 1967 and as an ambassador to Cuba from 1977 to 1980. She was also Director of Culture in her country and Director of the Regional Office of UNESCO for Latin America and the Caribbean. She has lived in exile in the United States since discovering her name on a death list compiled by paramilitary groups in Colombia; several persons on that list have already been killed.

Colombia: Another "Dirty War"?

Colombia is currently experiencing one of the worst crises of its history. The lack of security and the proven inefficiency of the judicial system are reaching terrifying new heights," said former president Carlos Lleras Restrepo recently. A prominent Liberal party leader, Lleras is not known for hyperbole.

With popularly elected civilian governments, a Congress and a free press, Colombia has long been touted as one of Latin America's few stable democracies. Paradoxically, it is among the world's most violent, with 15,000 homicides in 1986 alone.

Although U.S. press coverage has tended to focus on drug-related violence, narcotics account for only part of Colombia's turmoil. From 1981 to 1986, 3,547 journalists, students, teachers, trade unionists, members of opposition parties and civic organizations were assassinated, according to the Permanent Committee for the Defense of Human Rights (CPDDH) in Bogota. Widespread extra-judicial executions, disappearances and torture have left many here talking about a political "dirty war."

On October 11, 1987, Senator Jaime Pardo Leal, leader of the Patriotic Union party (UP) and presidential candidate, was murdered in his car outside Bogota. Riots erupted in the capital and several other cities, a general strike was called to protest the assassination and the military called out the troops. Pardo Leal was only the most recent of hundreds of members to be killed since the party was formed two years ago. (The UP itself estimates the death toll at more than 470; Americas Watch puts the number at closer to 250.)

Violence in Colombia is not new. In 1948, the assassination of populist leader Jorge Eliecer Gaitán sparked the bloody decade known as *La Violencia*, in which 200,000 were killed. Political violence later resurged under former president Julio César Turbay Ayala (1978-1982), who gave the military free rein. Under the aegis of the national security doctrine, a "security statute" was decreed, granting military and police forces full control over public order, and military jurisdiction over civilians. A staunch U.S. ally on Central American policy, Turbay presided over an era was that marked by extensive disappearances, torture and political assassinations.

The "Peace" Process

In this context, former president Belisario Betancur's (1982-1986) efforts to pacify the country through dialogue with guerrilla groups (of which there are currently six in the country) raised hopes that the violence might end. His peace program included a broad amnesty for rebels, cease-fire negotiations and the promise of economic reforms. Betancur's efforts to create a democratic opening did not receive the necessary support from Congress, the private sector or the press. Neither the military nor the guerrillas fully complied with the cease-fires. Human rights violations continued with impunity, and paramilitary activity—including disappearances and extrajudicial executions—increased dramatically.

The United States did not look kindly on Betancur's peace talks, much less his leading role in the Contadora initiative. In 1984, when U.S. ambassador to Colombia Lewis Tambs coined the term *narco-guerrilla*, it was understood as an affront and boycott of Betancur's negotiations. Ironically, the government later came to adopt the term to justify the tragedy at the Palace of Justice.

Indeed, Betancur's peace process collapsed in November 1985 when the M-19 guerrilla movement (named after the allegedly fraudulent elections on April 19, 1970) seized the Palace of Justice, taking hostage officials of the Supreme Court and Council of State. The military countered this attack with tanks and rockets, and the ensuing fire partly destroyed the building and its archives. Over 100 people died, including 12 Supreme Court magistrates.

In seizing the palace, the guerrillas demanded a "trial" of Betancur and his peace process, as well as the release of documents in the judicial archives which they claimed could prove that the military had consistently violated the agreements. Afterward, the government charged that the M-19 acted in concert with the mafia to destroy the files of drug traffickers facing extradition charges. The U.S. press embraced the claim.

Not reported, however, was that among M-19's hostages were members of the Council of State who earlier that year had ruled that Gen. Miguel Vega Uribe — Betancur's defense minister — was guilty of torturing at least one person during his tenure at the Institute of Military Brigades under the previous administration. Vega Uribe had repeatedly, and unsuccessfully, tried to reverse the decision.

The controversy following the "holocaust," as the palace tragedy is called in Colombia, forced Betancur to appoint a special investigative commission. A parallel independent inquiry was carried out by attorney general Carlos Jiménez Gómez. Although both committees agreed that the M-19 had not collaborated with the mafia in the operation, they differed strongly in their conclusions. The official tribune blamed the M-19 exclusively for the massacre, a finding called into question by ballistic reports which showed that none of the magistrates were wounded by M-19 weapons. The independent report denounced both Betancur and defense minister Vega Uribe for failing to make any effort to save the hostages. Jiménez argued that what should have been a rescue operation was conducted like a battle.

Whether Betancur delegated the responsibility of the operation to the military authorities, or whether the operation was initiated without his knowledge, remains unclear. What is apparent is that the "assault" on the Palace of Justice marked the resurgence of the military's political power.

Assassinations, No Assassins

In August 1986, President Virgilio Barco took office, promising a plan of "Rehabilitation, Reconciliation and Normalization" to promote economic and social development of regions in conflict. Although he has refrained from using force against the mass civic movements, extrajudicial executions — of which there were more than 1,000 in 1986 — have increased and changed in character under his government. As the Bogota weekly *Semana* noted, whereas the "dirty war's" victims were once anonymous peasants, students, workers and police, they are now well-known journalists, civic leaders, trade unionists and politicians — 99 percent of them leftist and democratic opposition figures.

The August 24 assassination of human rights leaders Hector Abad Gómez and Leonardo Betancur marked a new level of violence. The two were gunned down at the funeral of teachers union (ADIDA) president Luis Felipe Vélez, killed earlier that week. Abad Gómez's name had appeared — along with Jaime Pardo Leal — on a "death threat" list, released anonymously to newspapers and radio stations around the country. The list included Alfredo Vásquez Carrizosa, former foreign minister and president of the CPDDH; former attorney general Jiménez, and 32 other human rights activists, magistrates who have denounced torture, journalists who have condemned militarism, Liberal politicians, retired military officers, UP members and artists. The list represents "the overflowing violence against freedom of expression and criticism, with methods characteristic of a 'dirty war.' It is an essentially political and national problem," 22 of those threatened wrote in a letter to President Barco. Barco responded by admitting that there was "a macabre plan to destabilize the country."

Barco is not alone in his analysis. Economist Jorge Child, a columnist for Bogota's second largest liberal daily *El Espectador* — also blacklisted — wrote that "there is no longer any doubt that today we have paramilitary terrorism in cold blood... A type of violence unheard of in Colombian politics [dominated since the 1800s by the Liberal and Conservative parties]: the annihilation and extermination of a Leftist third party and of all people who denounce fascism,

McCarthyism, militarism and the 'dirty war.'" He added that the country might be on the verge of an anti-communist dictatorship similar to those of the Southern Cone under military rule.

For others, the origins of this subterranean war are not so clear. Fabio Echeverri, president of the powerful National Association of Industrialists, recognized that there is a "dirty war," but that "no one knows whether it's from the Left or the Right because there is no proof of who is responsible."

The UP, meanwhile, has charged that the Army is directly implicated in the killings and has designed the "Condor Plan" to "assassinate hundreds of members of the Communist Party (CP), the UP, trade unionists and democratic leaders." In December 1986 it presented the attorney general's office with alleged proof of military involvement in crimes against UP members.

A Third Party's Threat

The UP was formed during Betancur's peace process, attracting guerrillas from the Communist Revolutionary Armed Forces of Colombia (FARC) who sought legal channels of political participation. Since its inception, the UP has suffered over 470 assassinations, 34 of them senators, congressmen, city council members and mayors.

Many analysts have linked the apparent war against leftists with the appearance of the UP on Colombia's political panorama, which considerably strengthened the Left's participation in electoral politics. In fact, the UP obtained 4.4 percent of the vote in its first national campaign for Congress in March of 1986—double that of any leftist party to date. It won three seats in the Senate, five in the House of Representatives and several more in the departmental councils and municipal assemblies. This fact obliged the government to name UP mayors in several towns.

In March of 1988, mayors will be elected for the first time. Designed to democratize the political process in a country long dominated by traditional party politics, this measure is feared by some not only because of the tenuous balance in public order, but also because it opens the possibility that Communists may gain power on a local level. Analysts calculate that the UP could win no more than 40 to 50 out of a total of over 1,000 municipalities, and many have suggested that the current state of terror might be geared to justifying the cancellation of these elections.

"An Orchestrated Campaign"

In addition to the UP, high level government officials and international human rights organizations have directly accused the armed forces of human rights violations. As attorney general in 1983, Carlos Jiménez Gómez denounced 59 active military members as belonging to the paramilitary organization, MAS. (Meaning Death to Kidnappers, MAS was formed in 1981 in response to the kidnapping of a leading mafia member's daughter by the M-19 in Medellin. There are now over 100 paramilitary groups in Colombia.) All of those who testified to military involvement in the MAS during that investigation have since been assassinated.

Like Abad Gómez and Pardo Leal, assassinations occur in broad daylight by hitmen who are never identified, much less detained. "It's very common in Colombia in recent years," wrote columnist Caballero. "There are assassinations, but no assassins." Impunity flourishes because of the inefficiency of justice, as well as out of fear of reprisal.

Amnesty International has implicated the military in extrajudicial executions and disappearances. "Death squad gunmen openly carried military weapons in the presence of uniformed troops and police and traveled in military vehicles or unmarked cars with license plates — some of which are seen parked in police and military compounds. . .and were sometimes seen handing over prisoners at military bases and barracks," wrote Amnesty in its 1987 report. Victims testified that they had been detained and tortured by police and military personnel, in many cases identified by name. Given military jurisdiction over the cases, these abuses have continued with total impunity.

The military has responded with angry defenses of the institution. The High Command recently denounced an "orchestrated campaign" by the "enemies of Colombia" to discredit the armed forces and destabilize the country. And they have roundly rejected the possibility of investigating charges made against them or of submitting to trials in civilian court.

Self-Defense Groups

Meanwhile, Defense Minister Gen. Rafael Samudio has sponsored the formation of "self-defense" groups – equipped with Army-issue Israeli weapons – to defend themselves against "communists, guerrillas and the UP." Former minister of justice José Manuel Arias Carrizosa (forced to resign in September of 1986 over a scandal concerning illegal business dealings) also supported the measure.

This official support for peasant vigilante groups touched off a heated polemic, laying bare the tensions between militarists and non-militarists within the current administration. Ministers of interior and finance, César Gaviria and Luis Fernando Alarcón, and presidential adviser Carlos Ossa Escobar – in charge of Barco's pacification plan – were opposed. Barco has not commented on the self-defense groups, even though they clearly contradict his pacification policy.

According to the Fifth Forum for Human Rights held in Bogota last April, the armed forces continue to advocate military action as the best way to control public order and are supported in this by powerful corporations, the leadership of the Liberal Party, and the Bogota daily *El Tiempo*. Indeed, Defense Minister Samudio recently requested a $64 million hike in the military budget, which would raise it to an all-time high of $313 million, equal to one third of the national budget. Samudio's request was reinforced by a contrived flare-up over an old border conflict with Venezuela, and the renewal of the FARC's* guerrilla activity, which put the government on the defensive. Although Samudio received the support of several congressmen, Finance Minister Alarcón dissented, insisting that

---

*FARC: Revolutionary Armed Forces of Colombia

the priority is "not defense, but attending to [Colombia's] severe social needs."

In Colombia, the power of civilian governments over the military has been progressively diminishing since Turbay's government as the same military actors continue to pull the strings. Turbay's torturer Vega Uribe was Betancur's minister of defense. And the ground commander at the Palace of Justice massacre, Samudio, has stayed on as the current minister of defense. Under Barco, then, parallel military power is growing and could, as some have suggested, lead Colombia directly, or by proxy, to military dictatorship.

Laura Restrepo
Colombia

Laura Restrepo was editor of the national politics section of the magazine La Semana *in Colombia. In 1984, she was appointed by President Belisario Betancur to the Commission for Negotiation and Dialogue. The Commission mediated between the government and the two guerrilla organizations that had signed a truce with the government. Her significant role and her deep knowledge of the causes of the failure of the peace process made her a target for death threats from right-wing squads. Laura Restrepo lives in Mexico and works as a journalist.*

The Shirtless Man

Peace negotiations had been reopened with the M-19 and had begun with the EPL. The Commission on Negotiation and Dialogue had been formed, and was already working with these two groups, and with another guerrilla group (ADO) that had decided to sign the peace treaties at the last minute. . .

The government, along with the guerrillas, decided that their negotiations would not be limited to a closed door business arrangement. They wanted to share their discussions with the rest of the country and, to achieve this, press conferences and public gatherings were organized. The guerrillas did not have the legal status that would allow them to come down from the mountains, so the peace commissioners got their hats, boots, cameras and first aid kits together, and went into the jungle. The guerrillas, in turn, traveled for days to get to the chosen towns. Both the men and women prepared *lechona* and wore their clean clothes to meet the Commission. It was agreed that during these meetings neither the guerrillas nor the army would play dirty tricks; it was also agreed that, at least for some time, there would be a cease-fire. The army had to leave the zone where the discussions were going to be held and could not take advantage of the situation. The guerrillas, in turn, could not take advantage of the absence of the army and conduct armed operations. There were cordial meetings planned where specific issues relating to the peace agreement were to be discussed, and where officials, politicians, priests and businessmen would be given the unique opportunity to become closely acquainted with the guerrillas, and vice versa, and where both groups would listen to each other and try to reach agreements by means other than arms. These meetings would be, above all, good will gestures, but they were also intended as small trials of the peace to follow. Some took place with minor inconveniences: an airplane was left without gas, a commissioner sprained an ankle, a harsh discussion on the subject of kidnappings ensued; other problems were more complicated.

For the first meeting with an M-19 delegation, a small township of Paez Indians in the department of Cauca, named San Francisco, was chosen. Iván Marino Ospina, a commander of the M-19, some of his men, and Antonio Navarro Wolff, fourth in ranking, and a group of his people, would be present. Also with M-19 was Andrés Almarales, a leader who was semi-clandestine. The Commission was represented by Bernardo Ramírez, a former government official, Monsignor Darío Castrillón, bishop of Pereira, Horacio Serpa, president of the Liberal party, and myself. We took off in a helicopter rented to a private company. When we flew over San Francisco, we saw that it was not full of guerrillas, but of soldiers. When we landed, an army captain asked for our citizenship cards and made us stay on a corner of the plaza—"While I find out what this is about," he said.

In a split second, we were enveloped by a cloud of Indians, children and dogs. They waited in silence for a show, like those who wait in line to enter a theater. The three nuns in town came close and, with whispers that revealed their Spanish upbringing, they informed us that the soldiers had arrived two days ago, that there were one hundred and fifty men, and that the night before, they had been asking people for their ID's and patrolling the nearby mountains.

"Ramírez Rodríguez, Bernardo. He says that he was a minister of government, and that the president sends him. . .Almarales Monga, Andrés, he was benefited by the amnesty. . .Castrillón Hoyos, Darío. He says he's a bishop. . ." We heard the captain transmitting the information from our citizenship cards over his radio.

An Indian came close and, looking the other way while kicking pebbles along the roadside, said, "The guerrilla is up in the jungle, half an hour away, but they won't come down because they know the soldiers are in town."

"Tell them we are going to Cali to solve the problem and that we will come back," Bernardo Ramírez replied.

We flew to Cali, and from the Palmaseca airport, the former minister called President Betancur and told him about the unexpected events. Surprised, the president called the minister of defense and asked him what was going on. The minister answered that the troops had gone to San Francisco because they knew that the M-19 had plans to dynamite the roads leading to the area. The president repeated the order to clear the area of troops. When we returned to the town, the soldiers were still there, but the captain, this time cordially, told us that he had received orders from his superiors to abandon the place.

We watched the soldiers pack their belongings in the trucks and leave the town. Afterward, we sent a message to the guerrilla group through Indians who knew how to find them. We went to the nun's cool patio to wait. We were given hot chocolate with maize *envueltos* served on an immaculate white table cloth that was better deserving of holy wafers than of *envueltos*. After three sips of chocolate we heard the sound of bullets in the mountain. Then we heard heavy shooting and the shouts of Indian women who reached our place out of breath. "They're killing each other! They're killing each other!" We questioned them and found out what was going on. For some reason, the troops, instead of leaving the town by the road they had used to enter it, had gone into the jungle, through a narrow path without exit that led to the guerrillas' camp. At that moment, a young Indian man was the only one who offered an intelligent idea: "The peace commissioners should come with me in the helicopter to find the area of combat so that they can try to stop the fighting."

After half an hour of flying around in circles, the Indian pointed to some white dots. "There they are."

While flying low, we distinguished people running to an open area. They waved handkerchiefs at the helicopter. We landed, and about one hundred exhausted, sweaty guerrillas surrounded us. We could hear intense combat nearby.

"Let them come closer and waste bullets, so save yours."

"Bolívar, your sword fights, yesterday, today and always!"
"Hand me a rocket with wire and batteries."
"Look, there he is behind that bush."
"Crawl!"
"Lieutenant Federico, is everybody there?"
"Fuck!"

Seconds later, a guerrilla, who seemed to glide on his long legs, introduced himself as Antonio Navarro Wolff. He was on his way from the west with his men to meet Iván Marino Ospina and his group when the bullets surprised them as they bathed in a river. Both groups got together in the midst of the fighting. Then a well-built man came, riding a mule and carrying a rifle across his shoulder. He shouted: "This is a dirty trick. We were heading to the town to talk with the Commission and the army came to meet us." He jumped off his mule and, waiting a minute to regain his composure, he said to Bernardo Ramírez, "It's a pleasure, I'm Iván Marino Ospina. I'm in charge of this." Without waiting for a reply, he proposed this to us: "The firing and combat must stop. Let's make a white flag and you can stand between the two fighting groups. We will stop our fire and you tell the army to do the same. To put it another way, if the Commission doesn't go there to negotiate, this whole thing will go to hell. You have to make another little effort for peace. . ."

Bernardo Ramírez accepted immediately and the guerrillas looked for a white rag to make a flag. The only thing that was white and big enough was the pilot's shirt. He took it off and tied it to the end of a stick. It was agreed that Horacio Serpa would stay with the guerrillas so that he could mediate in case the army decided to attack from behind.

With the self-assurance of a tank commander, Bernardo Ramírez started to walk energetically along the uneven path, toward the area of the shooting. With a safari hat over his wild gray hair, with his unbelievable mustache, and carrying the white rag as his shield, he looked like an explorer, or a prophet of salvation.

With the same air of decision, Monsignor Castrillón began to walk with Ramírez. The bishop's Roman collar, and the cross on his chest, made the scene look as if a crusade was taking place in the saintly mountains of Cauca. I left with them. Five minutes later, the shirtless pilot hurried to join us.

"You don't have to get into this mess if you don't want to, this was not included in the contract," the former minister said, but the man replied that this was a way of building a country, and that he wouldn't miss it for anything.

Bullets were buzzing nearby. Maybe we were building the country, like the pilot had said, but the scene was more like a "Three Stooges" movie. Thinking about it, we started to laugh uncontrollably. The more the bullets exploded, the more our laughter roared.

"We are the Peace Commission!" The former minister commented that he never thought we would end up shouting slogans. He insisted that we walk behind him for security purposes and we, in turn, insisted that his gesture was very gentlemanly, as well as pointless, and that it would be better if he raised the flag higher. After half an hour of walking, the bullets were hitting so close that we could see the dirt they lifted from the path.

"Holy Father, if you wish to take our lives as a contribution to peace. . ." said Monsignor, becoming serious, his head leaning down, his Roman collar a bit crooked and his black suit covered with dust.

"Well, Monsignor, maybe we won't give our souls to anybody yet," Bernardo Ramírez protested. Meanwhile the pilot was shouting hurrahs to Colombia and the peace process. Suddenly a shot, from not less than fifteen feet, thundered through our ears and like springs the four of us jumped into a ditch.

"Raise your arms and walk," someone shouted at us. We got out of the ditch, raised our arms and walked.

"You son of a bitch, throw that shit!" they screamed at Bernardo Ramírez, who was still clinging to the flag. He threw it.

Immediately, the sights of several weapons appeared and we continued like that along the path. On both sides of the path, through the trees and leaves, the silhouettes of several soldiers appeared, and finally, in front of us, we saw the captain who had welcomed us to San Francisco. Bernardo Ramírez asked him why this was happening and told him that the shooting had to stop immediately. The captain replied that could only be done if he got direct orders from his superiors and took Ramírez to the military truck so he could personally communicate his message over the radio. Meanwhile, we sat on the grass to wait for our legs to recuperate. From our spot, we could see Ramírez talking and gesturing. There was a puddle of fresh blood on the roadside from a sergeant who had been wounded. A soldier came to us, shook our hands affectionately and said, "I admire you for your courage."

"We admire you more for your courage," was our wholehearted answer, "we have only been here for a short while, instead, you risk your neck every day."

After fifteen minutes, Ramírez and the captain came back. The captain ordered his men to end the shooting. A few bullets were heard here and there, but after that, the silence was complete.

Mission accomplished, we said goodbye to the troop and went up the path to meet the guerrilla again.

Television journalists Olga Behar and Ana Cristina Navarro were also there. They had gotten together with Iván Marino Ospina the day before and were prepared to cover the meeting with the Commission. When we arrived, they had already recovered from the commotion of the shooting that had driven them to great lengths to save their necks. Cameraman Fernando Rincón, from the new program "24 Hours," had been able to film the whole scene while running or hiding behind the bushes. He was the first one to document for television the confrontation between the Colombian army and the guerrillas. (Months later he was awarded the National Journalism Prize for that job.) According to the testimony of the female journalists, the guerrillas had decided to wait on the outskirts of San Francisco because of the information they had received from the peasants. They knew the army was in town and decided to come down when they were told that the Peace Commission had returned and that the soldiers were leaving.

Around 9:00 p.m., when the army had definitely left, and the guerrillas and the commissioners had gone down to town, the meeting finally took place. It wasn't a big thing. The guerrilla officials were not very excited when they were asked their opinion of the democratic openness, and what their legal activities would be like when the cease-fire took place. Iván Marino did not look very friendly; he wouldn't put down his weapon for a single second. One of them justified their attitude: "When things happen as they did today, who can believe that this will end like a fairy tale?"

The night ended in a party at a bar called El Romance, where Bernard Ramírez, soaked with *aguardiente*, had an interminable discussion with Iván Marino, who—not even when he fell asleep on his stool—let go of his weapon. Meanwhile, the pilot, with his shirt on, euphorically toasted whomever crossed his path: "This is how History is made, brother."

Translated by Natalia López

Olga Behar
Colombia

Olga Behar is a university professor and a journalist. She has worked in radio and television, winning several national awards. We excerpt from Behar's history of political violence in Colombia, Las guerras de la paz, *a book which relies strongly on testimonies. After its publication in 1985, death threats forced Behar to leave the country. She lives in Mexico.*

The Thorns on
the Path

I am in Bogota attending a press conference. The date for the signing of the peace agreements is getting closer and I want to be present for the prologue. I tell the second in command of the M-19, Álvaro Fayad (now general commander): "When the date for the signing gets closer, give me a call at the television station, because I want to go up to the hills to come down with the guerrillas to Corinto or whatever place is chosen."

About a month later, the call comes. Fayad suggests that I attend the meeting of the Commission on Negotiation and Dialogue. I request permission to go a few days early to carry out my idea of filming the guerrillas going down the mountain—a reporter's whimsy—and he accepts.

We make a date to finalize the details. There Fayad insists that the reporters from the competing channel go with me. I answer with an emphatic "no" and suggest: "Offer them an interview with 'Boris.' That's a good scoop, they will like it, you will see. Besides, this meeting is the same as the next, but I want to go to the signing of the treaty in the department of Cauca (Corinto) and not in Huila or Caqueta." My idea was to march for a week with the guerrillas to the site of the signing; that's why I insisted on going to Cauca. The final list of those who would travel to the singular adventure of San Francisco included journalists Ana Cristina Navarro (Spanish television), Olga Behar ("24 Hours" newscast), cameraman Fernando Rincón and sound technician Miguel A. Carrión. A good crew for a mystery movie, no?

The second preliminary meeting with the guerrillas had been set for that day, August 5, 1984. (The first meeting had taken place in Cordoba with the EPL.) That morning we were toasting, with hot chocolate and bacon, the beginning of the dialogues with the Commission, which was arriving at that little village about which I had heard so much. A saint's name, part of the forgotten geography of Colombia: San Francisco, on the outskirts of the majestic Central Mountain range in the Cauca Department. But we were still an hour away from its nearest dwellings.

A young, vigorous peasant with a small mustache was walking up the steep path which led to the encampment. His silhouette got bigger as he approached us, under the burning rays of the awakening sun.

In the meantime, armed and uniformed youngsters carried out a variety of tasks. Amparo, Roberto's companion (Roberto was the captain killed in Corinto at the beginning of April) was sewing a pair of pants. A strange sight that one, of a woman from Caqueta, with a rider's hat and a pistol in her belt, and a rough needle in her hand.

Two youngsters were sweeping the entrance to the little house, while listening to the news on the radio. Fernando, an older man who had been with the liberal guerrilla, the ELN, and the FARC, and was now with M-19, sang out of tune, but with a commanding skill in his handling of the guitar, which some serenaders had abandoned the night before.

All of a sudden, the man was among us, agitated and nervous. He announced to Iván Ospina, the general commander, that the government troops were approaching and that they were pretty close to the foot of the mountain. The commander, in spite of what they say about him in the cities, was determined to keep the promises he had made: "We have a commitment with the Peace Commission and we are going to carry it out." And, he added, looking at us: "If there should be a battle, what are you going to do?"

He didn't have to wait long for the answer: "Well, we will film it, that's the only choice we have." We knew that we could stay on the mountain, but danger was secondary to the opportunity of such a scoop.

But the military command preferred to wait prudently, instead of moving up to confront the enemy. The group of about eighty men and women split up. "We will climb different mountains; one group under the orders of Commandant Gerardo Ardila will head for that hill across from us, and you, future 'war correspondents,' are going with me toward this side of the mountain," Ospina told us, half seriously, half in jest.

The climb was arduous. It had to be very quick, and to avoid problems, the guerrilla leaders told us to do the opposite of what we wanted to do: we had to march ahead of the group to avoid being left behind, even for a second. We marched for an hour, getting further and further away from San Francisco. When we got to the top, some youths began to dig trenches. We sat down to wait. I remembered that I had some chocolates and we shared them while the time passed.

Israel Santamaría, a worthy son of Jerico, Antioquia, took out his tape recorder and soon we began to hear tangos which he hummed.

Sitting on the grass, Iván Marino showed us his pistol. It was the size of a pack of cigarettes. "But it kills just like a big one," he said smiling when he saw our surprise, and he added, "It is a present from a minister of a friendly government, but I will not mention his name or nationality."

Suddenly, we saw a helicopter in the blue sky. "It is the Commission," said Ospina with some anxiety. From our height, the road to San Francisco looked insurmountable. He advised a cautious wait; shortly afterward, we saw the helicopter fly away.

"Olga, you know them better than I, could it be that they have not seen us and decided to go away?" asked the commander. I answered that in my opinion they were probably flying over to announce to the guerrillas that they were ready to carry out their commitment, or else, had gone somewhere close by, "but I have no doubt they will return," I insisted.

Then Iván Marino said, "If they come back, as soon as they show up, we will go down, regardless of what happens. If they meet their commitment, I will, too."

It was 11:00 a.m. when we heard the sound of the blades close to us. "Let's go down," was the order, and we began the quick descent, again, toward the encampment. Once there, Ospina asked one of his subordinates to call the guerrillas on the other hilltop, under Ardila's orders.

We each had a heavy load to carry. For the guerrillas, it was the camping gear, the rations and the rifles. For us, it was the cameras, lights, batteries, the battery charger and our own clothes. The Armed Command had asked us to take everything because the ideal thing was to wait for five days in San Francisco and then leave for Corinto for the signing of the cease-fire.

For more than an hour we climbed down through narrow trails, immersed in a heavenly landscape of green mountains and gray creeks. We discerned the football field, which indicated to us that the highway was close. The rest was the easiest: about half an hour's walk on the main road to the square where the peasants, today, would not put their coffee beans to dry so that they could join in the peace activities.

The guerrillas were singing. They abandoned the rigid regulations about military marches and mingled. Now we were walking behind, looking at heavy backpacks, bags and rifles which slowed down the pace.

Suddenly, a burst of machine gun fire. It was not a stray shot. It was an attack directed at us. Iván Marino Ospina took over the command and received the information from his advance guard: "There are about sixty men, they are soldiers shooting at us." The first steps were taken: "Rifles ahead, pistols and unarmed people behind." We journalists stayed halfway, to witness the drama.

Nobody abandoned his belongings, but we were all sorry we had taken them with us. We shouldn't have been so trusting. "A rocket with wire and battery," a boy was shouting. The crossfire was intense and the guerrilla column was at a disadvantage—there was no planning or willingness to do battle; there were too many people carrying small caliber weapons or no weapon at all—but nobody lost control.

Bursts of gunfire from machine guns, rifles and rockets, made a dramatic chorus which lasted an hour. The army must have been about half a mile from us. My cameraman was about three hundred feet from me, filming what that night, on television, gave us goose pimples. When it was shown on the evening news, we realized how dangerous it all had been for us.

In moments like that, one only remembers the survival techniques of combat and knows that if one observes certain rules it is possible to come out alive and, perhaps, unhurt, at least if there is no bombing. I asked Iván Ospina for a dark jacket to replace my red sweater. Then I followed his instructions to the letter, crawling and moving quickly through the clearings.

All of a sudden, I found myself before Israel Santamaría, who advised me: "Go to the rear guard with the unarmed people," to which I answered, "You can't be so unlucky that you would die here with me; therefore, I will stay and see if I learn something." I suspect that my risky decision made him trust me more. He accepted and began to give me instructions. We protected ourselves behind the wall of a little white house. From the railings, Israel aimed at something that moved in the distance. . . "I hit him; he fell back," he said happily, but the guerrilla did not have time to celebrate. Afterward, we found out that he had wounded an army lieutenant.

All the bullets were coming at us from the left. Suddenly, they came from the right side. "We are surrounded," everybody must have thought. . .at least that's what Santamaría and I thought. The guerrillas were getting ready to return the fire, when a peasant came to us running, and yelled, "Do not shoot, it is Navarro Wolff who is coming this way from the river."

At last Navarro had arrived. Israel explained to me that he was coming from the Pan American Highway. He was one day behind schedule and his people were beginning to worry.

There was a short silence. The shots were no longer heard. There were two possibilities: either the battle had ended, or the army was preparing a hard offensive. To avoid taking any chances, Iván Marino Ospina ordered the retreat: "Everybody up the hill, let's go to the football field, not one step forward, not one more shot. If there is no meeting with the members of the Commission, it will be the army's fault."

We began the slow, uphill march. After ten minutes everybody was sad, nobody was singing. At least nobody was hurt. Suddenly, we heard a noise from the sky and the helicopter appeared.

Iván Marino asked me, "Is it an army helicopter, what do you see?"

"It is the Commission's helicopter. Look, it is white, with stripes," I answered.

Immediately he gave the order: "Watch out, they might shoot," and further ahead, Gerardo Ardila was asking people to get out their white handkerchiefs and wave them. My cameraman got out his white towel, gave it to the guerrilla, who took it and raised it to the sky. The passengers in the aircraft understood the signal and they went toward the football field, at the end of the highway on which we were moving very slowly and heavily.

A few meters from us, Antonio Navarro appeared with his people. We greeted each other and continued the march. He told me that the troops had tried to attack them while they were swimming in the river, but at that moment Iván Marino Ospina's group showed up, and the army changed their "target."

Once in the football field, and after warm greetings, commissioners Horacio Serpa, Bernardo Ramírez, Monsignor Darío Castrillón and journalist Laura Restrepo discussed the talks with the commandants.

Ospina was blunt: "Either we talk down there, in San Francisco, or there will not be a preparatory meeting, because it would serve no purpose to do it in hiding. It has to be in front of the people."

This is the moment when the commissioners take courage and sticks and white rags (for which the courageous helicopter pilot offers his white shirt) and go down to negotiate the withdrawal of the military troops.

At noon they come back, after suffering attacks because the army mistook them for guerrillas, and they confirm that everything is quiet. We go down to San Francisco.

The town's hospitality made it possible for the talks to take place in a house across from the little park. In little baskets they bring us *empanadas*, in pots they bring us sweetened coffee, in dishes, rice and meat

When the serious business was concluded — the planning for the signing at Corinto — the music from El Romance seemed inviting and allowed commissioners and guerrillas to mingle.

At dawn all the guerrillas were sleeping in the park, the commissioners in the parish house, the reporters and cameramen in the pool hall. After a sweet cold water bath, I went to the nuns, who invited me to share coffee and bread with the commissioners. There, I had a serious discussion with Bernardo Ramírez, president of the Verification Commission. He remained convinced that the attack had not been deliberate on the part of the National Army, and he said that after having spent two days with the guerrillas, I had learned their language. I told him I didn't care what he thought, because that night he and all Colombians would see how things had been. I added: "Watch the '24 Hours' newscast tonight, and then we can talk." I have the impression that Bernardo Ramírez found out, by way of the telecast, that I was right; afterward, he would confess that as he was going down the path with the sticks and the white rags, the army had fired on him, too.

As we finished breakfast, we changed the subject. Upon leaving, I saw Laura Restrepo taking careful notes and requesting different people's versions of what had taken place, to present a report to the president.

When it was time to go back, the helicopter came to the square. Iván Marino's and Bernardo Ramírez' parting words were, "We'll see each other in Corinto on Sunday." Ospina promised to set out the following day, crossing Toribío and other towns.

To us, that guerrilla dream meant the possibility of obtaining some nice television footage. That's why we decided to stay and march with the columns: a five day march — which the friends of peace in that Cauca zone would join; it was a beautiful piece of news for the country.

The preparations began. From Telecom-San Francisco, the telegraph office, Ospina requested from Bogota blue, white and red flags and the decals he wanted to stick on the automobile windows. A peasant arrived with a note whose exact words were:

August 06/84
From: Military Commander
For: Iván Marino Ospina

The purpose of this communication is to let you know
that at this moment I am in the Telecom office at Toribio
with the aim of talking to you by telephone and clearing
up some doubts about which surely you can give me an
answer.

Signed,
C.T. Oscar Echandia Sanchez
Military Commander

Ospina went straight to Telecom to wait for the call. The office
of the Colombian Army wanted to know how long he planned to
stay with his guerrillas in San Francisco, so that he could leave his
troops in Toribio and avoid a new confrontation. Ospina answered
that he would stay only one more day, but that his exit would be
precisely through Toribio, and that he was making it clear to him, so
that both would take the necessary steps to maintain the calm.

But a few hours later, the army officer received a countermand:
To march toward San Francisco. The man sent the message and the
guerrillas ordered a speedy exit.

A four hour walk through a hellish zone, steep and very thick.
We camped on a very high mountain. The guerrillas went to sleep
hungry and thirsty. We, the reporters and cameraman, joined
Gerardo Ardila's encampment; he gave us sugarcane fudge from
Santander which he had received that very day from home. Night
was falling and the mosquitoes increasing, and they are worse
than bullets.

We woke up fighting the mosquitoes and listening to Antonio
Ibañez on Radio Caracol. Iván said goodbye—he was going to find
another route to get to Corinto, because the Toribio route, via the
highway, had been canceled.

Antonio José Navarro was in charge of the large group.

Another eight hour march toward Jambalo, but there were army troops everywhere, and it was hard to move. When, at last, we arrived at a little hut in the mountains, in the middle of nowhere, it was midnight. Navarro invited me to get warm by the fire where they made coffee.

There we talked. We were very sad. His goal of marching to Corinto by the normal route was impossible and the possibility of my making an interesting television show had vanished. They would have to march for twelve hours a day for six days to keep the appointment at Corinto, and avoid the army.

Then it was decided that I should return to Bogota and wait there. A journalist shouldn't be walking for seventy hours, dodging bullets, with no clear professional objective.

It took two nights to go down. The first night, we walked for eight hours to a field that was anything but romantic, full of bugs, and humid. The guerrillas accompanied us. When we were very close to the field, one of the guerrillas whispered: "The pimps, the troops are right there." And so it was, not more than two hundred feet away, we saw a quiet group camping. We turned back up the hill to make a four hour detour, through marshes and thick woods. We were pricked at every turn...it's the thorns of the road, I told myself, trying to give a larger meaning to our walk. There were the thorns that stung us as a painful symbol of Colombian reality.

It was dawn before we arrived at the desired field. We slept a couple of hours in the hut of a humble peasant who was not scared of the subversives' gear. At 8:00, the guerrilla on guard woke us up to continue our trip.

Five hours going up and down. "Alonso" helped me through some paths. Sometimes we had to hide, fleeing from the dog's barking that would give us away. The torturous path continued through a forest which seemed to have suffered the consequences of man's intervention; hundreds of logs blocked the way, and we looked like performers on a tightrope.

Finally, we arrived at our destination. It was afternoon, and we decided to sleep since the descent to Jambalo had to be at night. There were government troops, and the guerrillas who accompanied us were wearing green uniforms and were armed. The last descent was quick—hardly a couple of hours—and we were already close to the town. We hired a local bus to take us to the main square, where we were to take the intercity bus bound for Santander de Quilichao. There we heard the news about the despicable assassination of the physician Carlos Toledo Plata, which took place in Bucaramanga in the early hours of that 10th of August. We tried to find the closest column of the M-19, the one commanded by Carlos Pizarro-Leongomez, to find out his reaction to the event, and also whether they would sign or not.

We left for Rionegro, which was the trail we had for that column. Close to Corinto, we were detained by an army patrol who, at first, pretended that they did not know who we were, but who later told me, "We will not let you go because it was your fault that the battle of San Francisco appeared on television and the truth was known." I answered, resigned, "The truth hurts, doesn't it, Lieutenant?"

Bogota, October 1984
Sumapaz, January 1985

Translated by Emma Buenaventura

Claribel Alegría
El Salvador

*Born in Nicaragua in 1924, Claribel Alegría grew up
in El Salvador. She earned her B.A. degree in philo-
sophy and letters from George Washington University. She has published ten volumes of poetry, three
short novels and a book of children's stories. In collaboration with her husband, D.J. Flakoll, she has
published a novel, several books of testimony
and Latin American history, and a number of
anthologies.*

The Politics of Exile

Exile has long been one of the accepted occupational hazards of writers, professionals and politicians throughout Central America: a likelihood, under the military dictatorships that have existed in the area for the greater part of the 20th century, that is roughly equal to the chances of coming down with malaria.

In my own case, I was born in Nicaragua but grew up as a Salvadoran because my father, a medical doctor and Nicaraguan Liberal, was driven into exile by the U.S. Marines when I was only nine years old. He could never return, except clandestinely, because the Somoza dynasty placed a price on his head, and he died, forty years later, still in exile.

A good many years ago, I left El Salvador, but not as an exile. I went abroad to study, to learn other languages, to see the world. I never again resided in my country, but every year or so I would return for a few months to visit family and friends, to regain the essential contact with my roots. It was not until seven years ago that I learned I could not go back to El Salvador. Or, to be exact, I could return, but from what I was told, the chances of leaving with a whole skin were not encouraging. So yes, that makes me an authentic exile.

Since then, I have lived almost permanently in Nicaragua, which is also my motherland: a land of warm, generous people where I feel very much at home. Naturally, it is painful not to be able to return to

El Salvador whenever I feel like it, to be unable to feast my eyes on its incredible gamut of greens, to be prohibited from contemplating the giant *ceiba* tree that adopted me when I was a little girl, or from listening to the everyday speech of my people. But I realize that my anger, my resentment, is subjective, and that I would be falsifying if I told you I feel "exiled" in Nicaragua. Because of that, instead of speaking about my own experience, which is unimportant, I would like to talk about the true political exiles of my country: the refugees, the displaced, the dispossessed.

Today, twenty percent of my fellow countrymen fall into those categories. At least one million Salvadorans have fled the country or have been driven out in fear for their lives. There are 500,000 of them in the United States alone, where the Reagan administration is making intensive efforts, under a new, restrictive immigration law, to round them up and return them to El Salvador where they face internment in the army's new concentration camps, or death. More thousands are scattered throughout Canada, Mexico, the other Central American republics, and Europe.

Two years ago I talked with some of the new flood of exiles in a Sanctuary center in San Francisco, where there is an underground colony of some 300,000 Salvadorans, nearly all of them undocumented, and where an average of 300 per week were, even at that time, being hunted down by the *migra* — the immigration authorities — and deported.

The figures boggle the imagination, and the only protection these people have is the sheer weight of their numbers and their social invisibility in largely Chicano communities. So, let me focus on a single case — a typical story which I learned secondhand — a tale that you can multiply in your mind by a factor of hundreds of thousands. Let me tell you about Pastora, the child poet of Colomoncagua, a refugee camp in Honduras a few miles from the Salvadoran border.

Pastora is twelve, perhaps thirteen years old by now, and she told her story to my daughter, Patricia, who visited the camp as a member of a human rights delegation two years ago. Until she was eight, Pastora lived in the Salvadoran department of San Vicente, which is a disputed zone in the current civil war.

The National Guard swept through one day, in a typical "search and destroy" operation, and caught her entire family in their peasant hut. One of the soldiers knocked her mother unconscious with his rifle butt, another shot her father through the head and then killed her two small brothers, who were screaming, while Pastora, huddling in a corner under the bed, watched the carnage.

She and her mother managed to escape, hiding in a *tatus*, or manmade cave, until the last of the Guards had passed through. Little by little, other survivors of the massacre came out of their hiding places and, without burying their dead, commenced their exodus at nightfall. Their flight, in single file, toward the Lempa River which forms the border between Honduras and El Salvador in that region, was a nightmare that has been repeated thousands of times since then. It is known, with typical Salvadoran black humor, as *la guinda*, which means, "as easy as picking cherries."

When babies cried, their mothers would stop their mouths so the Guards wouldn't hear them, or offer them their dry breasts to stop their whimpering from hunger, thirst and fright. One small boy would not stop screaming until his father, in desperation, stuffed a handkerchief in his mouth, and he died of asphyxiation. During four terror-filled days and arduous nights of forced marching, they followed the banks of the Lempa, nourishing themselves on roots and leaves and an occasional wild berry. During the days of hiding, helicopter gunships patrolled overhead, firing rockets at anything that moved. At night, the adults took turns carrying the wounded in makeshift litters.

On the morning of the fifth day, a detachment of Guards appeared ahead of them, cutting off their retreat, and they were forced to cross the river into Honduras. Those who could, swam across. The others clung to rotting logs, and someone had brought an inner tube and a rope for such an eventuality. There were more deaths at the crossing: a number of small children, some of the wounded and one pregnant woman.

It has been five years now since Pastora arrived at Colomoncagua. A schoolteacher at the camp taught her and the other children to read, and she in turn taught her mother and is now teaching smaller children and adults the elements of literacy. As if that were not enough, Pastora developed the poetic itch. She writes poems about her dead father and brothers, about the importance of learning to read (the illiteracy rate in the encampment has dropped from eighty to less than thirty percent), about the threatened resettlement in El Salvador that the refugees dread. She began to write rhymed verse without anyone teaching her, and when she writes about the New Society, her words take on a prophetic ring.

She sent me half a dozen of her poems with Patricia—a fraternal gesture from one poet to another—and I had them published in a Managua literary supplement. Much, much later, Patricia wrote me that another human rights delegate had personally delivered the published poems to Pastora, who was delighted—as any poet would be—at her early recognition.

A few months after Patricia recorded Pastora's story, a company of Honduran soldiers burst into the Colomoncagua encampment on a mission of terror and intimidation. The attack took place at 3:00 p.m. on August 29, 1985, and I have read the detailed eyewitness accounts of the atrocity, disseminated by the El Salvador Commission on Human Rights on September 5, 1985.

I can only imagine that Pastora must have witnessed this second nightmare from another hiding place. According to multiple accounts from international observers in the camp, there were five Salvadoran soldiers and one North American Green Beret guiding the Honduran troops in a hunt for specific victims. I will not go into the gory details, graphically described in the testimony. Two people were killed, one of them a two-month-old baby who was kicked to death by a Honduran soldier. Thirteen were seriously wounded by gunfire, and twenty-five others were savagely beaten with rifle butts. Two women—one of them the schoolteacher—were repeatedly raped in the schoolhouse, and ten men and boys were captured and led away to a waiting helicopter, never to be seen again.

This is typical of the human suffering resulting from what the U.S. Pentagon laconically calls the Doctrine of Low Intensity Conflict. The "low intensity" presumably refers to its minimal effects on U.S. and international public opinion. But for Pastora and her fellow victims, the intensity is maximal and mortiferous.

The Salvadoran army is waging total war against its own people, with the expert advice of hundreds of U.S. military advisors and the logistical and economic support of the Reagan administration. The same holds true for its next-door neighbor, Guatemala, except that the military advisors there are Israelis. These are quiet little wars that have dragged on for years without receiving much attention in the international news media. There are no body bags being shipped back to the United States with the remnants of American boys inside them. Congress can be counted on to give President Reagan any amount he says he needs to continue the war, now that the death-squad killings have dropped to about one a day and the Salvadoran military have President José Napoleón Duarte as their civilian front man.

Perhaps few have heard about Operation Phoenix, which took place little more than a year ago in the Guazapa area of El Salvador.

Operation Phoenix: the name has macabre overtones since the Vietnam War, when it was the code name for a CIA terrorist operation, run by former CIA director William Colby, that slaughtered 30,000 civilians who were suspected of being Vietcong sympathizers. This new Operation Phoenix used ten percent of the Salvadoran army, including three elite battalions and the Salvadoran air force, to kill or drive the civilian population out of a 1500 square kilometer area covering Suchitoto, Aguilares and Guazapa. The soldiers applied "scorched earth" tactics to the entire area, killing civilians, burning huts, destroying animals and crops. The air force rained a ton of bombs daily for more than a month on the densely-populated area, and the army troops followed with a "mopping up" operation to clear the area of all signs of life. An undetermined number of civilians were killed and some 500 were captured and taken off to relocation camps.

What is the strategic objective of these Phoenix-type operations, which have taken place at regular intervals for the past five years? In counter-insurgency parlance, they are aimed at "taking the water away from the fish"—that is, taking the civilian population away from the guerrilla forces to deprive the latter of support. After a guerrilla zone has been properly "scorched" and depopulated, the government plans to resettle it with concentration camps containing displaced persons from other zones of the country who have been investigated, cleared and issued identification documents which they must carry at all times. The army controls all aspects of life and seeds the camps with informants to report on suspected guerrilla sympathizers.

This Orwellian militarization of society has worked better in Guatemala than it has thus far in El Salvador. The illiterate indigenous population of the Guatemala highlands is less politicized than the wily Salvadoran peasant, and the so-called Guatemalan "poles of development" are reportedly packed with the widows and children of men who were slaughtered in the savage counter-insurgency operations that Ríos Montt launched in 1982.

In El Salvador, however, with its dense population, the "water" — the people — stubbornly flows back to surround the "fish." The *guinda* has become a way of life for the people of Guazapa, who have survived approximately twenty such army forays during the past five years. The civilian population melts away before the army advance, each column of refugees led by guerrillas who know the direction of the army's thrust, and circle around it to wait until the armed forces have completed their work of devastation before flowing back into their ravaged territory to start rebuilding and replanting.

Displacement camps and exile are a deliberate strategy of the doctrine of low intensity warfare. The Guazapa peasants are intermittent refugees on the very land they till. Pastora has been exiled for five years within a few kilometers of her own country. As for the 500,000 Salvadoran exiles being hounded out of the United States under President Reagan's new immigration law, I have only this to say.

When they refurbished the Statue of Liberty in New York harbor recently, I hope someone had the common decency to take down the bronze plaque engraved with Emma Lazarus' poem:

> Send me your wretched and your poor,
> your huddled masses yearning to be free. . .

Lady Liberty may be holding high her torch "beside the Golden Door," but in her other hand, these days, she holds something that looks suspiciously like a whip.

IV.
Sparks of Fury and Shooting Stars:
Poetry

Pastora
El Salvador

Pastora is a twelve-year-old Salvadoran girl. She was eight when forced to seek refuge in a camp in Honduras. Her father and two small brothers were killed by the military. She learned to read in the refugee camp and taught children and adults. We have lost contact with Pastora.

The People's Teachers

Every single one of the instructors
We work without complaint
we aren't better
than the community here.

We aren't intellectuals.
Because we know how to share
right now in these moments
we want to make some suggestions

Well, we instructors
have an obligation
to be good conductors
of the new generation.

The way to teach
is to have lots of patience
to teach with love
all scientific knowledge.

Teaching these days
is an education

partnership, because here in the camps
life is communal.

Every single one of the instructors
We work with determination
doing this we are examples
for the new generation.

Translated by Andrea Vincent

Construction

We refugees
don't have an education
but here we are working on
the basis of cooperation.

We have ourselves, new workshops
and centers for nutrition
and with the effort of everyone
we are constructing education

So many things to address
in our new society
we want to see progress
living in fraternity

Translated by Andrea Vincent

Alaíde Foppa
Guatemala

*Alaíde Foppa was born in Barcelona, Spain in
1915 and raised in Italy. In 1944, she traveled to
Guatemala and met her husband. She decided to
adopt Guatemalan citizenship. In 1954, after the coup
against Jacobo Arbenz, she went into exile in Mexico.
Alaíde has said, "Rather than history, my life is
geography."*

*Alaíde was a founder of International Women's
Association Against Repression in Guatemala
(AIMUR), FEM, a major Latin American feminist
publication, and Foro de la Mujer (Woman's Forum),
a radio program in Mexico. She has raised five
children and published four books of poetry. In
December of 1980, she was kidnapped by the army in
Guatemala, where she had gone to visit her elderly
mother. Alaíde Foppa is still disappeared.*

from "Words"

I

An infancy
nourished on silence,
a childhood
sown with partings,
a life that seeds absences
From words alone
I expect
the ultimate presence

II

I expect almost everything
from words
not even knowing
what they promise
or deny me,
what lies beyond
the echo they strike.
I do not know
whether they are born on my lips
or whether someone is prompting me
in a mute language
whose code I cannot crack

Alaíde Foppa

III

Perhaps I hide
in words, to cloak
my nakedness;
perhaps
they keep stripping me
down to the last
dissembling veil.

V

Why do I write?
Because I'm alone
and my voice might startle me?
Because I'm waking
from a confused dream
that I can't remember?
Or just because I confront
a blank page
and there's a lump in my throat?

VII

Poets always speak to someone.
With sword or wheat sheaf
They address the people
or sing softly
to a loved one,
revealing unexpected
dazzling scenes.
Their path is strewn with flowers.
But in my dark retreat
I bear poetry
like a secret disease,
a hidden

illicit fruit

XII

A poem
was born this morning
in the clarity of the air.
My mind wandered,
and it slipped from my hands.

XIII

I wish I could say everything
in a few ordinary words
and if I said *apple*
fresh colors would shimmer
in mid-air
acid flavors
balanced forms
memories
symbols.
But is the word necessary
if the apple exists?

XV

Words are not
the ones that speak:
they say almost nothing,
they cheat.
But a hidden voice
whispers behind them
and familiar words
suddenly stun.

Alaíde Foppa

XX

A long silence
from far away
enters me slowly.
When it dwells in me
and all other voices
are stilled,
when I am nothing
but an island of silence,
perhaps I'll hear
the longed-for word

XXI

Of all this endless
shedding of leaves
that is time,
of the entire journey
of lost seasons,
of all this laborious weaving,
what shred will be left
intact, untorn,
what submerged island
will remain for the saving word?

XXII

Song is too much.
A word
would be enough
spoken in a soft voice,
suspended in air,
a word
that barely brushes the skin,

leaving a faint trace
in time.

XXVI

I must not lose
this grain of salt
this seed
this spark of sun
this strange kernel
this gold dust
between my fingers
this nostalgia
for what never was
this secret stem
this word
that an unknown hand—
now perhaps mine—
attempts to write.

XXVII

Stripped
day by day
of all my garments,
dry naked tree,
in my solitary withered mouth
fresh words
will still blossom

Translated by Rozenn Frère and Dennis Nurkse

Woman

Woman,
unfinished being
not the remote angelical rose sung by poets of old
nor the sinister witch burned at Inquisition's stake
nor the lauded and desired prostitute
nor the blessed mother.
Neither the withering, taunted old maid
nor she who is obliged to be beautiful
Nor she who is obliged to be bad
nor she who lives because they let her
Not she who must always say yes.
Woman, a being who begins to know who she is
and starts to live.

Translated by Margaret Randall

Julia Esquivel
Guatemala

Born in 1930, Julia Esquivel, an elementary school teacher, studied theology in Costa Rica. She has directed the Instituto Evangélico de América Latina (Evangelical Institute of Latin America) and founded the Comité Pro Justicia y Paz (Committee for Justice and Peace). She also started the publication of two magazines: Cristo compañero *and* Diálogo. *Her book of poetry,* Threatened with Resurrection: Prayers and Poems By an Exiled Guatemalan, *was published in the United States.*

They Have Threatened Us with Resurrection

It isn't the noise in the streets
that keeps us from resting, my friend,
nor is it the shouts of the young people
coming out drunk from "St. Paul's" bar,
nor is it the tumult of those who pass by excitedly
on their way to the mountains.

There is something here within us
which doesn't let us sleep
which doesn't let us rest
which doesn't stop pounding
deep inside,
it is the silent, warm weeping
of Indian women without their husbands,
it is the sad gaze of the children
fixed there beyond memory
in the very pupil of our eyes

which during sleep,
though closed, keep watch
with each contraction
of the heart,
in every awakening.

Now six of them have left us,
and nine in Rabinal*,
and two, plus two, plus two,
and ten, a hundred, a thousand,
a whole army
witness to our pain,
our fear,
our courage,
our hope!

What keeps us from sleeping
is that they have threatened us with Resurrection!
Because at each nightfall
though exhausted from the endless inventory
of killings since 1954**,
yet we continue to love life
and do not accept their death!

They have threatened us with Resurrection
because we have felt their inert bodies
and their souls penetrated ours
doubly fortified.
Because in this marathon of Hope,
there are always others to relieve us
in bearing the courage necessary
to arrive at the goal
which lies beyond death.

They have threatened us with Resurrection
because they will not be able to wrest from us

---

*Rabinal: town in the province of Baja Veracruz where a massacre took place.
**1954: year in which the government of President Jacobo Arbenz was overthrown by a CIA-backed army coup which initiated the ever-mounting repression by the military regimes in power since then.

Julia Esquivel

their bodies,
their souls,
their strength,
their spirit,
nor even their death
and least of all their life.
Because they live
today, tomorrow and always
on the streets, baptized with their blood
and in the air which gathered up their cry,
in the jungle that hid their shadows,
in the river that gathered up their laughter,
in the ocean that holds their secrets,
in the craters of the volcanoes,
Pyramids of the New Day
which swallowed up their ashes.

They have threatened us with Resurrection,
because they are more alive than ever before,
because they transform our agonies,
and fertilize our struggle,
because they pick us up when we fall,
and gird us like giants
before the fear of those demented gorillas.

They have threatened us with Resurrection
because they do not know life (poor things!).

That is the whirlwind
which does not let us sleep,
the reason why asleep, we keep watch,
and awake, we dream.

No, it's not the street noises,
nor the shouts from the drunks in "St. Paul's" bar,
nor the noise from the fans at the ball park.
It is the internal cyclone of a kaleidoscopic struggle

which will heal that wound of the quetzal
fallen in Ixcan.
It is the earthquake soon to come that will shake the world
and put everything in its place.

No, brother,
it is not the noise in the streets
which does not let us sleep.

Accompany us then on this vigil
and you will know what it is to dream!
You will then know
how marvelous it is
to live threatened with Resurrection!

To dream awake,
to keep watch asleep,
to live while dying
and to already know oneself
resurrected!

Geneva, March 8, 1980

Parable

You ask me, my sister,
how have I made it this far?

It was really very simple,
to begin with
they removed one of my arms.

The man who thought himself most qualified
pulled the hardest.
He wanted to appropriate for himself
the very life force
which gave my arm strength
and movement.
In this way, he imposed on me
his macho rights.

It was the same arm
with which I had fraternally
shared with him
Light and Bread
when he was once in great need.

He had decided
to overcome me
with that blind obstinacy
we women know so well

While the others,
standing by neutral,
watched
with "cold objectivity"
and concluded
that a woman's arm
was of no importance.

From the force exerted
the joint began to give way
until the limb parted from my body,
while the others,
still neutral,
watched until
the mutilation was complete,
choosing to keep
their united male silence.

Alone with God,
I dried my tears.
The hemorrhaging slowly stopped,
but the pain lasted for centuries.

Suddenly this New Arm
was created
strong and pliable
like freshly baked bread.

And my heart?
I'll tell you:

As I was sleeping peacefully,

I dreamt of friendship and joy.
But an icy cold penetrated my whole being
and the pain awoke me.
In that tunnel of death
I lived through the horror of hell

While I was still dreaming
they, the same ones,
ripped out my heart
and took off with it like booty

They left behind
only that which they thought useless.
They took away everything
except the Spirit,
which they were incapable of seeing.
From it life was reborn,
a new path was opened up
and the darkness
became Light for me.

So I have experienced all of it
from the scandal of the Cross
to the joyous surprise of Mary Magdalene.
Sometimes weeping,
sometimes singing.

With the heart of my people
burning in my breast,
I have regained Life,
and with it the Future.
Like you, Guatemala!

1975, 1977

Dolly Filártiga
Paraguay

Dolly Filártiga was born in 1956. In 1976, her brother Joel, then seventeen years old, was tortured and killed by the Paraguayan police. Dolly was forced to see his mutilated body. The Filártigas initiated a lawsuit, but after receiving many death threats, they decided to leave the country and settle in the United States.

Joel's assassin also came to this country. That prompted another lawsuit by the family. The rule in this case, favorable to Dolly and her parents, is a historic decision in a U.S. court. It severely fines the criminal; however, it sets him free. Dolly shares her feelings in these poems, while she continues working for human rights.

Guaraní* Anguish

all at once died my flesh and soul
joel life of my life murdered without my hand at your side
the shout of vengeance in our father
dragging your body i am bled dry of tears
while our mother her eyes vacant disbelieving
pushes me torn and sobbing to battle the enemy
always the memory of your dead-child smell
goes with me in the sleepless nights delirious
i look for you to tell me again your pain
to name for me the cowardly torturer
as a sister and a woman i want to find him
to wipe out his life and his diabolical face
never to stop cursing all his breed
going my way here in the anguished northland
i save all my love for just your face

Translated by Regina M. Kreger

---

*Guaraní: Indian group, native of Paraguay, Brazil and northeast
Argentina

Always the North

this northland so immense and so vacant
the very one that shelters the assassins of my people
lends to me also its courts and its judges
that I might find comfort accusing my brother's killer
the show over he goes free its law smiles on him
my only comfort (and that of the tortured dead) that god will
     punish him
through it all exiled in this land and confused i
analyze the whole murderous lie invented by the keepers of power

Translated by Regina M. Kreger

María Gravina Telechea
Uruguay

*María Gravina Telechea was born in Uruguay in 1930
and studied at the University of Montevideo. She is
a French teacher who, because of her political
activism, lived in exile in Chile and Cuba. She won
the Casa de las Americas award for her poetry. She
has three children.*

November 8

an earthquake I want
or you to be transformed
into a lover of mine by the sun
like you were once and the stars

I have to hold you somehow

today I kiss your ridiculous
and kiss your miseries
and kiss your daily evasions
and cry and insult and love
and want
not only your truth shivering me
but all your greys and dotted lines

never nobody disloved me so strong to the bone

Translated by María Negroni and Sophie Black

Since

y our sister I am
for those issues of fog
and aim
since you put my screams into words
and if I keep talking like this
against the rain
it's because there are butterflies
stubborn in not dying now

Translated by María Negroni and Sophie Black

The bird flew flew

I lose the weapons
how I laugh at my hands
holding four winds
and not even an orange!
and no gun!
bad times after all

Translated by María Negroni and Sophie Black

Cecilia Vicuña
Chile

*Cecilia Vicuña was born in 1948 and studied at the
University of Chile and in London. As a poet and
artist, she was openly identified with the revolutionary process curtailed by the military coup in 1973
After the coup, she decided to remain in England. She
published six books of poetry. She lives in New York,
where she is the editor of a series of Latin American
literature in translation.*

Wikuna

Wikuna* being
is grazing & running

A white breast
at day's end

A sprout on the peak
exploding

Wilderness in a body

Eyes overflowing
a little head

      *

Woolly flower
slipping bv

I sleep
in your domain

---

*Wikuna: animal, much like the llama, found in the Andes·

Cecilia Vıcuña

Lose my head
& go back to find it

Wikunanessence
of wikunatv

*

Thought
as perfect light

Filament
piercing crystal

Fiber of prayeı

Geometry
unexpected

& suddenly there

*

You who eats
and scrapes

You who are
escapes

Restorer
of meaning

The strength
between us

The animal
rising
from our love

*

Our Lady of the Andes
jump

You are my
hot stuff
potato head

My whoops
clunk

You are the Cupisnique

The Uru
and the Bamba

What are you doing

The Apu here
gold on the mountain
and the Rimac there

What are you doing

Wikuna on the mountain
three clear snorts
three sharps she's off

Frugal wild

Effervescent
fountain of wool

Rug in the sun

Daughter and mother
of a better time

Cecilia Vicuña

Now you're oft
and your legs
are thunder

You wanted it
ordered it suffered

Why am I you?
Be Wikuna and graze

Take your rug
north and south

For what
pepper pot?

Why have you come?

Translated by Eliot Weinberger

Topac Inca Yupanqui

T opac Yupanqui wanted

The rasping songs
the words smooth
and golden
as the skin of a shell

Topac Yupanqui wanted them

Waiting
for that barren wind
that body
full of sun

He loved them
stitching that cloth
woven from water

That constructed
saliva

Wind in the inner
mountains of the palate

Cecilia Vicuña

Yupanqui watches it go by
as thunder
as a waterfall

He watches it
feeding on syllables
on missed opportunities

It flies by his mouth

Yupanqui wants it
hopes to possess it
hold it in his mouth
a stone
inside his skin

He chews it savors it
consummates it gives it back
to let it be

The song reappears
floating evasive
so that nothing
no one
may possess it.

Translated by Eliot Weinberger

Sachaj La Numac
Tiox Mundo

Pardon my sin God Earth,
I am borrowing for a moment
your breath and also your body.

— Divining prayer, Maya Quiché

And Tiox Mundo came
to forgive our sins, our
squandered breath,
the ruined word
at the bottom of the sea
where everyone weeps
and no one,
no one!
hears their tears.

Bodies abandoned
by their motion,
smiles abandoned
by their light,
eyes abandoned
by their sight—
against their will!

Cecilia Vicuña

With violence
for neither light
nor movement wished
to go.
The mouth still
wished to smile,
the eyes to see,
but one came who
didn't care
or didn't listen to
the eye's desire
or the will of sight.

One came who
slashing, silencing
broke the strength
tore the threads
that held the corners
of the mouth,
one came who
with raised fist
interrupted the prayer.

Translated by Magda Bogin

Jacinta Escudos
El Salvador

Jacinta Escudos was born in 1961 in El Salvador, and lives in exile in Nicaragua. Her poetry has been published in Mexico, Nicaragua and the United States. Letter from El Salvador, *her collection of poems, was published in England. She has written a short novel.*

San Salvador 1983

This is how I see myself,
forever running through the streets with the ghosts
of my San Salvador,
although nostalgia
takes over so easily
because the city will never be the same
when we get to know her again.
Despite everything
(your lead-pocked and silent walls,
your splatters reminiscent
of prehistoric murals,
your inhabitants who come and go
and all of us),
despite everything, I say,
your lights tucked away
in far-off valleys will keep their sparkle
like diamonds of a necklace
and your people, like *zompopo* ants,
running counter to the vague letter of decrees,
against the lethal eye contact
and mutual distrust.
Being subversive will be
having the willpower to kiss someone

with all the tenderness of the world
>DON'T LET THE BULLETS MESS UP YOUR SOUL, MY
>LOVE,
and don't forget the beginnings
the great genesis that created this situation
>YOUR WAR-TRAINED HANDS CARESSING MY HAIR

This is how I see myself,
far away being born and reborn
with the mouth full of old poets,
unknown but truly mine
>LET THEM BURY ME NAKED
>WHEN PEACE COMES, MY LOVE.
and with thunder detonating and rats and trains
surging through my hands,
and in between the scars they left on me
spikes of that city so deep in sleep
that neither the kisses
of a thousand princes,
nor a thousand market women,
nor a thousand statues
will be able to awaken
>THE RAZORS SLITTING YOUR EYES, MY LOVE
and I,
so anonymous
my name is never mentioned
(because mentioning names can be prohibited),
I'm with the usual swallows and vultures,
funeral processions,
the Gerardo Barrios Plaza,
the cathedral and Presidential palace,
the ubiquitous wicked haunts,
nameless spots
where collective rage
sets off jokes and diversions.
>THEN YOUR HANDS, MY FACE, YOUR LIPS,
and everyone shouting and applauding

from the innards of this great phantom
which is now my San Salvador,
    MAGGOT OF A CITY, BUT I DO LOVE YOU
as never before and forever
with the dust and scorching midday suns
little cafes and important decisions,
Oh what a country, how can you even exist!
    BUT I LOVE YOU
with your curlicues and feathered crest,
the beautiful and respected national colors,
the sky and sea
so blue
    LIKE THE FLAG THAT WRAPS YOUR CORPSE
and photographers
on top floors of all your buildings
your streets like arteries
or rivers
    LIVING, NOT JUST MAKING IT.   !
Oh, specter of a scary city!
    BUT I LOVE YOU

Translated by Zoë Anglesey

Caly Domitila Cane'k
Guatemala

*Caly Domitila Cane'k was born in Guatemala. A
social worker, catechist and teacher of literacy in her
Indian community, she also coordinated a Catholic
radio program in Cakchiquel, her native language.
She came to the United States as an exile after three
of her brothers, one fourteen years old, were killed or
disappeared by the military*

Birth and Death

Bells that sound slowly in myself
like drops of rain,
sounds that do not stop
for the mourning of the bells,
for the mourning of life for death
Today my little brother's birthday
a day of sadness for my family
Seventeen years ago
Narciso Gabriel was born.
Three years ago he was tortured
by the fog,
by my country's murderers.
Today only poetry tells the story
of our lives,
the sufferings of many in Latin America
Bells that never stop sounding,
sounds that are witness to our crying.

Today I tell and write
the passion I bear in my firmament
the cross
the memories of an injustice.

Birth is happiness
death, grief and mourning.
The dreams of life have been wounded.

Today, only an illusion
of the brothers I had:
Only wounds from their existence,
bells sounding from Earth to Heaven,
bells singing from life to God,
from pain to prayers,
from death to resurrection.
Today their faces are changed to drawings and poetry,
I no longer see them,
I do not touch them..
Defying the control of the system
our days will brighten
different horizons.
Today His blood is the seed.

Translated by Regina M. Kreger

Candles

Lit candles
light new candles.
Extinguished candles
still will light new candles.

Thus is struggle:
candles that light
and fade.

Translated by Regina M. Kreger

Presa*

Prisoner, pressed,
today and tonight,
at sunrise and
the next day.

This silent moment
underneath the sunset,
sounds awaken me,
from within and outside myself.

Prison,
the presence of each one
of my brothers,
my companions.

I find myself pressed,
I don't understand the people's language,
I don't understand the words to the songs,
I only understand the precious vibrations of my guitar,
she is my friend,
I play her when I am alone,
she keeps me company with songs
when I cry,

*Woman in Prison

Caly Domitila Cane'k

I hug her when I wake up in prison,
my guitar with me in prison,
prisoner of pain

Papa and Mama

When I see your faces in the portraits
of those shadows,
my soul sobs,
my heart pounds,
I sigh for pain,
for happiness,
for the immense space and
void that separates us.
We hold back the tears in each other's eyes.

I feel lonely.
I walk along
carrying the pain of evil,
which is like the heat of fire
that whips our souls,
empty of mourning for death,
for the martyrdom of enduring hunger and
the cold wind of poverty.
I sob for the wreckage
of the very rites of the breath of life.
I want to see you.

Translated by Regina M. Kreger

Alenka Bermúdez Mallol
Guatemala

Alenka Bermúdez Mallol was born in Santiago, Chile. She became a citizen of Guatemala, the country of her husband and children. One of her children was killed in combat in Guatemala. Alenka lives in exile in Nicaragua, where she represents the Alaíde Foppa Guatemalan Cultural Workers Association

I Want to Explain a Few Things...

To my children and all the children still with us,
I want to explain a few things;
Just to tell you, for example,
that fires, grenades, machine guns
are necessary, real, needed,
because, how can we win this battle
relying upon geraniums and roses?
Of what use is song that remains but song?
Of what use unless it bursts forth in rifles,
blossoms into plows, then books?
That is why, children, I want to explain a few things,
lest you fear the final bullet

Translated by Alicia Partnoy and Sally Hanlon

I Take Your Hand and Move On

I take your hand and move on
into the future.
(Sunlight in my heart
when I used to say "I love you.")
And your skin in communion with mine
pouring all the love in our blood,
pouring the brushwood, the whole sea;
and I walk to the heart of life,
perfumed with countryside for you,
cleansed by spring water for you,
and I wear the stars in my eyes
and I set the moon upon my hair
and honey and balsam I gather in my hands,
and wheat lends me
its bright ripeness.
I become
fleece, moss, clear water,
guitar, dove, earthen jar
And I become
nightfall, noon, daybreak,
and I escape
riding the winds toward
your lifestream

Translated by Alicia Partnoy and Sally Hanlon

Reyna Hernández
El Salvador

Reyna Hernández was born in El Salvador in 1962. She studied at the School of Arts in San Salvador. At the age of fifteen, she enlisted in the guerrilla movement, where for nine years she took part in their actions. Captured by the military, she spent one year in jail. Reyna lives in exile in Sweden where she studies linguistics and literature

There Will Be Someone

Who doesn't like it

My heart
became a clown
this afternoon
    It danced
      It hissed
        It scatted
and it broke in two
at the feet of the abandoned
the blacks and Latins
                the indigenous
Also the thief and the prostitute.

Translated by Zoë Anglesey

In Old Man Shoes

You will remember me
short on words
eyes that saw to the marrow
My hand
this one
the strongest,
the one that knows how to do everything
is dreaming a dream.
The moon
is crying
and a tear falls on me
looking for my heart.

In shoes of an old tired man
nowhere did I leave
footprints

Sorry

Translated by Zoë Anglesey

Etelvina Astrada
Argentina

Etelvina Astrada was born in Germany in 1930 and grew up in Argentina. Her oldest son was disappeared by the military in the late seventies. She went into exile in Spain. Etelvina published several volumes of poetry. Her poems have appeared in the Massachusetts Review *and the* International Poetry Review, *among other journals.*

The Hordes Came

For Roberto Jorge Santoro

The hordes came
and sacked homes, towns, cities —
    they seized control of the living and the dead,
day, night, hopes, dreams,
the wind, rain, forests,
calendars, hands, books,
parents, children, grandparents.

The hordes came,
created darkness
and terror,
the hunt
goon squads
kidnapings
walls
interrogations
olive green
transfers
extermination camps
voltages
water torture
saws
gaffs
mutilations

231

dogs and rats
gnawing flesh and guts
and thus the dead were created,
the dead
dead
in the streets, on rooftops, in factories,
in schools, offices, on doorsteps,
in churches, in jungles, in the sea,
in barracks, in prisons.

The hordes came
and put through legal channels the death
of:
Pedro, Luis, José, Graciela, Alicia, Diana,
Julián, Oscar, Miguel Angel, Thelma,
Raimundo, Haroldo, Rodolfo, Roberto,
offspring of all the children, friends of friends,
extended families
and the missing among the missing.

The hordes came
with their flies neat and buttoned up.
Three polluted asses
and a single face truly sinister.
Three professional buzzards
sitting on the despot seat
in this time of funerals
and what good eggs they lay
hatching perpetual crimes.
Beneath the nation's flag
under the boot everything goes,
even the sky goes underground.
These are the military virtues we have to endure!

Translated by Zoë Anglesey

In My Country

In my country
you can't choose to die of natural causes
or when you want to die.
In my country
death is not a biological act.
Childhood just suddenly stops, no more growing up,
therefore the young will not retire in old age
nor will the elderly get older still.
In my country
you do not carry the cause of your fatality in your blood
nor is death predicted by oracles
nor does it happen like fate striking,
only a single blow to the neck
without rhyme or reason
pointless, colorless, flavorless.
In my country you die
before you slip on a phony peel
so therefore
chance, good luck no longer exist.
In my country
nothing is permitted
not even being a corpse,
laid out beautifully,

immensely poetic and immortal,
or thinking death to be personal,
as property, our very own and private.
Likewise to be easy going is out,
being slow or stubborn,
we are not permitted to master at least
that anonymous passing away in the hospitals
or the dying in a homely fashion
as it happens in other parts of the world
assuming a modest guise in the halflight
on an antiseptic bed, tended to by our family,
rocked by the crying of our own survivors.
Nothing is permitted us,
not a bit of insanity,
choosing bars over any window
or knotting the noose like Nerval did.
In my country
death is a pestilence,
but it's not pus, leprosy, gangrene,
punishment from heaven
in seven plagues.
It's a sickness much more serious,
extremely so,
it's a worm in the neurons,
the testicles,
the heart.

My country
is Death,
a gigantic assassin, omnipotent with power,
magically evaporable,
minus the stench,
a death with dead
but lacking corpses.
Thus in my country
there are no gravediggers,
elegies go unsaid,

Etelvina Astrada

no one buys a little snippet of eternal peace.
The dead are not laid to rest.
In my country
you can't hear the toll of bells for the dead,
personal demise as a custom
is a thing of the past.

Translated by Zoë Anglesey

V.
Setting Distance
on Fire:
Letters

Verónica de Negri
Chile

*Because of her political activities, Verónica de Negri
was imprisoned and tortured by the Chilean military
after the 1973 coup. She came to the United States as
a refugee. Verónica de Negri was very active in the
human rights movement when the Chilean military
killed her son, Rodrigo Rojas, burning him alive in
Santiago. The assassinaton of Rodrigo in July 1986
only gave her more strength to fight for justice. She
travels extensively, denouncing human rights violations in Latin America. Verónica now lives with her
son, Pablo, in Washington D.C., where she works as
a counselor for youth, families and battered women.*

*This letter was written to Lilian, also the mother
of a victim of repression. It follows the return to Chile
of Lilian's surviving son, a close friend of Rodrigo
and Verónica.*

Dear Lilian

Washington D.C.
October 10, 1987

Today I will only let flow those feelings strongly rooted in me. Thanks for your letter and thanks for all the support, love and care you provided me during my days of torment in Chile in July 1986. I want to tell you that I have thought of you so often in the past, and when I think of you today, I think of the Calvary, and understand the horrendous loss of a son.

We have suffered these losses because there exists in Chile a condition that has destroyed the lives of our sons, the lives of the great majority of our people, our lives. When your surviving son, my friend, returned to Chile recently with his wife and child, I felt my family breaking apart again. I lost another part of my Rodrigo, because they were the closest physical presence that reminded me of him. I think I told your son, "I'm happy that your mother will have her two sons close to her now."

I know it seems crazy, but the fact of being able to take flowers to the cemetery is very important. The torture of not being able to go to the cemetery has great magnitude; now, I understand the relatives of the disappeared...I, at least, hold the hope of returning one day, when there will be no obstacles for me; but not even in that bright future, will they learn what happened to their children, where their children rest...We must be so strong!

I love you all so much, especially your son and daughter-in-law, because they are very honest, they haven't lost their dignity, a dignity your son seems to have inherited from you, and that his wife owes mainly to her fight for survival as a young woman who believes in justice. "Justice," a word that unfolds for us many questions. What is justice? Will we see it someday? Of course, we will and we do. I grew up knowing it, and I'm positive that even when the military and all their security forces do not grant us the justice of written laws, we are—in one way or another—doing our dead children justice. When your son offered tribute to Rodrigo, he was also doing justice to his own assassinated brother. Both cases are so similar. We also do our children justice by living the way we do, by fighting with strength and dignity.

Dear Lilian, I would like to tell you so many things, but my heart is closed. .The admiration I feel for you, for all of you, has helped me continue walking this path whose length is still a mystery. We only know that it will change, that the next one will be bright, green, a flourishing path. We have earned it.

A warm hug and all my love,

Verónica

Clara Piriz
Uruguay

Back in Uruguay after many years of exile in Holland, Clara Piriz has recently worked in the organization of the "Uruguayan Women's Plenary."
*   The letter she shares with us was her first uncensored communication with her husband, who had been a political prisoner in Uruguay for twelve years.*

Marriage by
Pros and Cons

Abcoude, Holland,
May 12, 1984

Dear Kiddo,
 I'm writing this letter with no margins, without counting lines, or pages, without measuring my words a damn bit. Our first communication uncensored and uncut.

 The big question is if I will manage to write without self-censorship. . .internalized censorship. Fear. My fear of causing you pain, of showing myself as I am, of confusing you in my confusion . . .My fear of losing what I've gained and gaining what I've lost. . .

 A while ago I wrote you that it would be good for you to try to get out with a passport that would allow you to come and go. Let me explain why. At bottom it just has to do with another fear: the fear of ruining your life. . .even more.

 Living in exile is a bitch. "Sure," you say, "it can't be worse than prison." True, prison is much worse. But, there is one fundamental difference: In prison you have to use all your energy to survive in a situation that doesn't depend on you and that you can't change. To survive in exile you have to use all your energy to change a situation of terrible inertia and, if it changes, it will be only because of your personal effort.

 You arrive here with nothing, no friends, no job, no house, no family. You don't understand the system in which you've somehow got to function. The place assigned to you is marginal, socially, economically, politically, culturally, emotionally. No one gives a damn about you. You have no history. Or rather, the history you have, no one cares about. Although suddenly it occurs to some reporter to use you as material for an article. A monkey in the zoo. And you accept, of course, because it's part of the political work: call attention to Uruguay, get political pressure. But if you achieve anything, no one cares. There are too many people. Most of all there are too many foreigners. Discrimination exists, and it is rough. It sucks to feel looked down on, it sucks to have to do twice as much to get credit for half. It sucks when you say something and they look at you: *"and where did you crawl out . . ."* Not to mention worse things, like insults and violence.

But not all of it comes from outside of us; a lot we bring on ourselves. Most of the exiles resist adapting. They don't want to be here; they didn't choose to come to this country; everything is going wrong for them. The Dutch "smell bad"; *"you know how they are."* The exiles don't want to learn this fucking language, they refuse to give two and be counted for one. *"What for, anyway, if I'm going to leave . . ."* Result: Many of them have ended up completely screwed. Ten years of doing nothing of any worth, always running around, drinking beer and Geneva gin. Some of them read a lot, they remind me of your brother, a vagabond with books under his arm. Others have made a way for themselves, working like mules. Some have had the advantage of having studied, others of being stubborn workers with the "nasty habit of earning their living." This small group has one other problem: We are isolated because there's not enough time and energy to work, learn the language, etc. . . and still maintain friendships scattered all around the country.

A while ago I was talking with two Chileans and an Argentine woman I see regularly (a recently found remedy for the isolation). They said that even though they work, speak Dutch and have Dutch friends, communication with them had a limit they couldn't cross. I've heard that from other people. I must confess that is not the case with me. I have good friends who are Dutch, with whom my communication is excellent.

Well, as you see I'm not painting you a very pleasant picture. I can imagine that after twelve years in jail all this seems banal, but experience shows that once you are here the twelve years of jail don't help you think, *"What a terrific time I'm having."* On the contrary, those years are one more problem.

In your case, there might be some points in your favor. Supposing our relationship works out (another subject altogether), I have made a way that can make your adjustment easier.

You might ask yourself if I am telling you this to try to discourage you. No. What it means is that I know what you'll have to face if you come here. And I don't want to have it on my conscience that I lured you with a siren song.

Our situation is not very encouraging either: two years of living together in very abnormal conditions. Twelve years without seeing each other: you in jail, which has certainly changed you. Neither one of us knows what problems are going to crop up from that. Certainly, within normal limits, you've changed a great deal. But it's also logical to expect less normal changes. There is no superman who can come unscathed out of one of those places. I don't believe those people — and there are some — who come out saying, *"Prison? A great experience, it's nothing."* I also have lived through very hard experiences; I also am very much marked.

Besides, as a couple we're going to face a very strange situation. I have matured in this country, I have carried out a whole process of learning, of critical integration, of getting situated here, which you, one way or another, will have to carry out. This puts you in a position of dependence on me, which does not contribute to a healthy adult emotional relationship.

I'm finishing this letter today, June 24. Happy birthday! After yesterday's phone conversation I have such anxiety to see you, to talk to you, to touch you, that I can't imagine how I'm going to live from now until we see each other.

Yet there's so much we will have to discuss and go through!

And don't get all romantic on me and tell me that love, or the will to love, can overcome everything. No. It can overcome a lot, it is an essential condition, but not enough. I've seen so many who could not withstand the pressures of the change.

From a very young age, I have been bothered by rules without reasons, by *just because* or *because I said so* or *because that's the way it has to be.* It has bothered me as much in my social as in my private life. And systematically I have created a new set of rules based on my own experiences, on their analysis and synthesis and also on the reading and studies of the ideas of other (wiser) people. This attitude toward life is not new for me. Just think, if not, Carolina would not exist. Carolina was not an impulse, a mistake, a transgression. For me she was a conscious moral act which I have never regretted.

It was not always so easy: For years I struggled inside myself. Because sincerity is one of my values, at times I had to choose between the risk of destroying you or lying in the gentle way, by keeping quiet. Sometimes I kept quiet, sometimes I didn't. Finally I arrived at a formula: I'd try to let you know as best as possible how I felt about a lot of things and avoid the details that could be painful for you.

But my evolution is not only in that area. Most important to me is my maturity and my independence. That's why I made that comment on the phone yesterday: "You are going to have a hard time with me." I don't like to be ordered around, or told what to do. I reaffirm my right to my own decisions, your right to your own decisions, our right to be and think differently.

When I stayed alone with the girls I had to perform all of the roles; I was their mother and their father and their pet dog, too. I got used to it and from there I chose what I liked best to do, and that's not necessarily the womanly duties. Therefore (referring to a fantasy you wrote me about that frightened me): If you want homemade ravioli, make them yourself. I'll help you eat them. And I'll drink the wine. As a housekeeper I am consciously a disaster. My work is much more important to me, and my personal and professional development more than anything. For years my possibilities were limited by the urgency of moment to moment life, and by the girls' ages. Nevertheless, I got started with a brave effort. Now they are grown, they have their own independence, they're not attached to me, and I have found a phenomenal job. You can imagine that I'm grabbing onto that with all my strength. At my age it's my last chance and I can't and don't want to miss it.

We don't know what each of us means by a "primary relationship." You said it very blithely, as if there was a universally accepted formula. But I am certain that it's not that way. When I was twenty years old, I believed it, but not now, and that is not disillusionment, not at all, it's wisdom.

For instance, you asked me if I had a boyfriend. You didn't know how to deal with my answer. You said that could surely be the biggest stumbling block, and I answer you that the stumbling block is not that he exists. . . but the fact that *I* am capable of having a boyfriend.

I hold that I have been relentlessly faithful. Perhaps not in the way that you mean, but I'd bet if we talked about it, you'd see my way is much better.

Why do I want to see you? Because I do. Because I also allow myself the right to be (every once in a while) compulsive. I'm doing fine, I have a good job, a good social life, a serene and comforting relationship, the girls are growing up with no problems. Then why create problems for myself? Why not leave things as they are? Because I want to see you. Because I would feel terribly frustrated not to see you, because it would be a lack of respect for you, for me, for what we were, for what we are, and perhaps for what we might become. . . Because I want a second chance. Because only you and I can decide if it'll work or not. That decision is not for time, or distance, much less for the military to take. It's ours.

On the phone I found it hard to say I love you, for fear you misunderstood what I felt. So, I'll say: In my own way I love you. We'll have to see if my way and yours will meet — and grow.

Bye,
Clara

Translated by Regina M. Kreger

Carmen Batsche
Guatemala

Carmen Batsche was born in 1945. When she was nine years old, her mother was exiled from Guatemala and the whole family settled in Argentina. Batsche is a human rights activist and has three children. Her sister disappeared in Argentina in 1976 and, in 1982, her mother, who had returned to Guatemala, also disappeared at the hands of the military.

Dear Alicia

Buenos Aires
July 22, 1987

Let me introduce myself through this letter. I'm the daughter of Maximina Valdez, disappeared in Guatemala City on September 9, 1982, under the government of Efraín Ríos Montt. My sister, Norma Leticia Batsche Valdez, disappeared in the Republic of Argentina on December 15, 1976, under the government of General Jorge Rafael Videla. I live in Argentina because my mother found asylum at the Argentine Embassy in 1954. That is why I write to you from this country where I have my home.

My mother, my father, my sister and I—all Guatemalans. I was three years older than my sister. We traveled with my mother, who came as an exile to Argentina. At that time, we had just lost the wonderful democracies of Arévalo and Arbenz, two great presidents of Guatemala. My mother was active in politics and, when the government fell, we had to leave the country. Here in Argentina, Perón had decided to bring the families along with the exiled. My sister and I came with my mother. My father came later.

We started the fight to make our home in this land. My mother and I suffered a lot; we wouldn't adapt. But my father and sister felt very comfortable here—my sister considered herself an Argentine to the point of fighting against the military dictatorship and being disappeared in 1976.

In 1966, when we applied to become permanent residents,

something shameful happened. There was a discussion that made us feel very bad. We, the girls, were considered to be under political asylum; it was absurd that two children who had come at the ages of six and nine could be under political asylum. Well, that was our case. We didn't think that it was bad to be under asylum, but we believed that the immigration authorities were acting in an extremely wrong way.

After our arrival in Argentina, we were kept in the Hotel for Immigrants, where they used to house all new immigrants. Each time we entered or left the hotel we had to go through a check point. Afterwards, each family found their own place. The Eva Perón Foundation helped us a lot with wood, beds, mattresses. But the absurd thing was that many exiled men were detained in the Villa Devoto prison. My mother, along with the people from the Liga Lucha por los Derechos del Hombre (Fight for the Rights of Humankind), the only organization that helped the political prisoners, used to visit the detainees. I crossed the bars to the side of the prisoners. My mother visited them for more than a year, until they were all released. They were given ID's, they had to check in with the authorities every month, and renew their ID's every six months.

This story is to show you how the "yankees" can control a constitutional government, and never leave it free to do its will. It is a hard fight, that of the people who want to achieve real freedom of thought, speech and action. I say goodbye now,

Carmen

Buenos Aires
September 24, 1987

Dear Alicia,

I received your letter; I had been wondering whether you had received mine. I am glad to know you did and am glad to be again in touch with you. I will try to answer some of your questions.

I learned about your project though the Fedefam* newsletter. I felt the urge to write you, and I followed my impulse.

---

*Fedefam: Federation of Relatives of the Disappeared; coordinates all Latin American relatives' groups.

249

About the kidnapping of my mother: I denounced it to the Inter-American Commission for Human Rights, the Fedefam, and here in Argentina, to the organization of the Relatives of Political Prisoners and Disappeared. I go to the Mothers of Plaza de Mayo's march every Thursday, and the last time I was in Guatemala, I reported the case to the GAM (Mutual Support Group).

My mother disappeared on September 9, 1982 at 12:30 p.m. from the market where she worked, along with a young woman. I received a telegram with the news on September 12, and I traveled to Guatemala, leaving my three children by themselves. The smallest was then three years old, my daughter was six, and the oldest was ten. I was in Guatemala for a year and a month asking presidents Efraín Ríos Montt and Humberto Mejía Victores to tell me where my mother was, but they always denied having her. Sick, sad, and with vanquished hopes, I went back to my children, who in that year, had managed on their own as best they could. I found in them the strength to keep living.

I'll tell you about my mother. She was a very strong woman who had to fight since she was a child. She knew about everything; I mean, she really knew what misery was and she fought, day by day, to better her life. She was extremely kind, honest and hard working. I admire those qualities in her and it's not just because I'm her daughter that I say this, she really had those virtues... She liked politics from the bottom of her heart, she carried politics in her blood. I know that only death could stop her from getting involved in politics. She always opposed injustice. She was a true fighter, very committed, very courageous. I admire even the way she quit smoking. Once, she had to undergo surgery. She used to tell us that when she left the operating room, a nurse came frequently to lend her a cigarette for a puff or two. When the nurse left, my mother had to spend two hours without smoking. She was desperate. But she realized that if she could spend two hours without cigarettes, she could spend her whole life without them. Then she quit.

I could tell you so much about her. She was available at any moment to work for peace. When I was a little girl, she made me collect signatures for peace.

... [My mother] never wanted to get married. My father always wanted to marry her, and I even asked her to marry my father. She never paid any attention to our requests.

My sister's name is Norma Leticia Batsche Valdez. She disappeared on December 15, 1976. She was in her fourth year of medical school and had a little girl who was then two years and nine months old. They captured the child's father two weeks after they captured my sister. The girl is now twelve years old. We denounced the kidnappings to the Inter-American Commission for Human Rights and to the Mothers of the Plaza de Mayo. The writs of *habeas corpus* my mother presented always received negative replies.

Well, Alicia, I wanted to be brief, but it was impossible. I hope I was clear. If you have any questions, write back and I'll be pleased to answer them. I wish you good luck in all you do. Receive a warm hug from

Carmen

Translated by Alicia Partnoy

Selected Bibliography

Anthologies

Anglesey, Zoë. *Ixok Amar·Go: Central American Women's Poetry for Peace*. Penobscot, Maine: Granite Press, 1986.

Boccanera, Jorge. *Palabra de mujer*. Mexico: Editores Mexicanos Unidos, 1982.

Manguel, Alberto. *Other Fires: Short Fiction by Latin American Women*. New York: Clarkson N. Potter, Inc., 1986.

Flores, Angel and Kate Flores. *Poesía feminista del mundo Hispánico*. Mexico: Siglo XXI Editores, 1984.

Randall, Margaret, ed. *Women Brave in the Face of Danger*. Trumansburg, N.Y.: The Crossing Press, 1985.

Silva-Velazquez, Caridad and Nora Erro-Orthman. *Puerta abierta: La nueva escritora latinoamericana*. Mexico: Joaquín Mortiz, 1986.

Contributors' Publications

Acebey, David. *Aquí también Domitila!* Mexico: Siglo XXI Editores, 1985.

Agosín, Marjorie. *Conchali*. New York: Senda Nueva de Ediciones, 1980.

-----. *Hogueras*. Santiago: Editorial Universitaria, 1986.

-----. *Los desterrados del paraíso, protagonistas en la narrativa de María Luisa Bombal*. New York: Senda Nueva de Ediciones, 1983.

-----. *Pablo Neruda*. Translated by Lorraine Ross. Boston: Twayne Publishers, 1986.

-----. *Scraps of Life*. Trenton, N.J.: Red Sea Press, 1986.

-----. *Silencio e imaginacion: metaforas de la escritura femenina*. Mexico: Editorial Katun, 1986.

-----. *Witches and Other Things*. Trans. by Cola Franzen. Pittsburgh: Latin America Literary Review Press, 1984.

Alegría, Claribel. *Album Familiar*. San Jose: Editorial Universitaria Centroamericana, 1982.

-----. *El Detén*. Barcelona: Lumen, 1977.

-----. *Flowers from the Volcano*. Translated by Carolyn Forché. Pittsburgh: University of Pittsburgh Press, 1982.

-----. *Luisa in Realityland*. Translated by Darwin J. Flakoll. Willimantic, Conn: Curbstone, 1987.

-----. *Nicaragua, la revolución sandinista: una crónica política, 1855-1979*. Mexico: Ediciones Era, 1982.

-----. *No me agarran viva. La mujer salvadoreña en la lucha*. Mexico: Era, 1983.

-----. *Para romper el silencio: resistencia y lucha en las cárceles salvadoreñas*. Mexico: Ediciones Era, 1984.

-----. *Pueblo de Dios y de Mandinga (Con el asesoramento científico de Slim)*. Mexico: Ediciones Era, 1985.

-----. *Sobrevivo*. Havana: Casa de las Américas, 1978.

Alegría, Claribel and D.J. Flakoll. *Cenizas de Izalco*. Barcelona: Seix-Barral, 1966.

Astrada, Etelvina. *Autobiografía con Gatillo*. Madrid: Ayuso, 1980.

-----. *Muerte Arrebatada*. Barcelona: Ambito Literario, 1981.

-----. *Poesía política y combativa argentina*. Madrid: Editorial Zero-Zyx, 1978.

Barrios de Chungara, Domitila with Moema Viezzer. *Let Me Speak! Testimony of Domitila, A Woman of the Bolivian Mines*. Translated by Victoria Ortiz. New York: Monthly Review Press, 1978.

Behar, Olga. *Las guerras de la paz*. Bogota: Planeta, 1985.

Burgos, Elizabeth. *Me llamo Rigoberta Menchú y así me nació la conciencia*. Mexico: Siglo XXI Editores.

Dujovne Ortiz, Alicia. *Buenos Aires/Seyssel France*. Paris: Editions du Champ Vallon, 1984.

-----. *El Agujero en la tierra*. Caracas: Monte Avila Editores, 1983.

-----. *El buzón de la esquina*. Buenos Aires: Editorial Calicanto, 1977.

-----. *Wara, la petite indienne de l'Altiplano*. Paris: Larousse, 1983.

Esquivel, Julia. *Threatened with Resurrection: Amenazado de Resurrección*. Brethren, 1982.

Foppa, Alaíde. *Las palabras y el tiempo (Words & Time)*. Flushing, NY: La Vida Press, n.d.

Gambaro, Griselda. *Conversaciones con chicos: sobre la sociedad, los padres, los afectos, la cultura*. Buenos Aires: Ediciones Siglo Veinte, 1983.

-----. *Dios no nos quiere contentos*. Barcelona: Lumen, 1979.

-----. *Ganarse la muerte: novela*. Buenos Aires: Ediciones de la Flor, 1976.

-----. *Lo impenetrable*. Buenos Aires: Torres Agüero Editor, 1984.

-----. *Teatro*. Buenos Aires: Ediciones de la Flor, 1984.

-----. *Teatro: Nada que ver; Sucede lo que pasa*. Ottawa: Giral Books. 1983.

Letelier, Isabel and Michael Moffit. *Human Rights, Economic Aid and Private Banks: The Case of Chile*. Washington/Amsterdam: Institute for Policy Studies, 1978.

Martínez, Ana Guadalupe. *Las cárceles clandestinas de El Salvador*. Mexico: Casa El Salvador, 1979.

Menchú, Rigoberta. *I, Rigoberta Menchú: An Indian Woman in Guatemala.* ed., intro. by Elisabeth Burgos. Translated by Ann Wright. London: Verso, 1984.

Partnoy, Alicia. *The Little School: Tales of Disappearance and Survival in Argentina.* Pittsburgh/San Francisco: Cleis Press, 1986.

Peri Rossi, Cristina. *Descripción de un naufragio.* Barcelona: Lumen, 1975.

-----. *Diáspora.* Barcelona: Lumen, 1976.

-----. *El libro de mis primos.* Montevideo: Marcha, 1969.

-----. *El museo de los esfuerzos inútiles.* Barcelona: Seix-Barral, 1983.

-----. *Evohe.* Montevideo: Giron, 1971.

-----. *Indicios pánicos.* Montevideo: Nuestra América, 1970.

-----. *La mañana despues del diluvio.* Gijon, Spain: Nogera, 1984.

-----. *La nave de los locos.* Barcelona: Seix-Barral, 1984.

-----. *La rebelión de los niños.* Caracas: Monte Avila, 1982.

-----. *La tarde del dinosaurio.* Barcelona: Plaza y Janés, 1985.

-----. *Lingüística general.* Valencia: Prometeo, 1979.

-----. *Los museos abandonados.* Montevideo: Arca, 1968.

-----. *Una pasión prohibida.* Barcelona: Seix-Barral, 1987.

-----. *Viviendo.* Montevideo: Alfa, 1963.

Restrepo, Laura. *Historia de una traición.* Bogota: Plaza y Janés, 1986.

Telechea, María Gravina. *Lázaro vuela rojo.* Havana: Casa de las Américas, 1979.

Traba, Marta. *Above and Beyond.* Munich: Starczewski, 1971.

-----. *Arte en Colombia. Art in Colombia.* Washington: Ediciones de la Unión Panamericana, 1960.

----- *Arte latinoamericano actual*. Caracas: Ediciones de la Biblioteca de la Universidad Central de Venezuela, 1972.

-----. *Camas, Feliza Bursztyn*. California: Museo de Arte Moderno la Tertulia, 1974.

-----. *Conversación al sur*. Mexico: Siglo XXI Editores, 1981.

-----. *Dos décadas vulnerables en las artes plásticas latinoamericanas, 1950-1970*. Mexico: Siglo XXI Editores, 1973.

-----. *El museo vacío*. Bogota: Ediciones Mito, 1958.

-----. *Elogio de la locura*. Bogota: Publicaciones del Museo de Arte Moderno, 1984.

-----. *En cualquier lugar*. Bogota: Siglo XXI Editores, 1984.

-----. *En el umbral del arte moderno: Velazquez, Zurbaran, Goya, Picasso*. San Juan: Editorial Universitaria, Universidad de Puerto Rico, 1973.

-----. *Historia abierta del arte colombiano*. California: Ediciones del Museo La Tertulia, 1973.

-----. *Historia del arte: El Barroco*. Bogota: Ediciones Universidad de Los Andes, 1967.

-----. *Historia natural de la alegría*. Buenos Aires: Editorial Losada, 1951; Losada, 1952.

-----. *Hombre americano a todo color*. Caracas: Editorial Arte, 1975.

-----. *Homérica Latina*. Bogota: Carlos Valencia Editores, 1979.

-----. *La jugada del sexto día*. Santiago: Editorial Universitaria, 1969.

-----. *La pintura nueva en Latinoamérica*. Ediciones Liberia Central, 1961.

-----. *La rebelión de los santos*. San Juan: Ediciones Puerto, 1972.

-----. *La zona del silencio*. Mexico: Fondo de Cultura Económica, 1975.

-----. *Las ceremonias del verano*. Barcelona: Montesino Editor, S.A.; Ediciones Norte, 1981.

-----. *Los cuatro monstruos cardinales*. Mexico: Ediciones Era, 1965.

-----. *Los grabados de Roda*. Bogota: Ediciones del Museo de Arte Moderno, 1977.

-----. *Los laberintos insolados*. Barcelona: Seix-Barral, 1967.

-----. *Los muebles de Beatriz Gonzalez*. Bogota: Ediciones del Museo de Arte Moderno, 1977.

-----. *Los signos del silencio (José Luis Cuevas, Francisco Toledo)*. Mexico: Colección Testimonios del Fondo. Fondo de Cultura Económica, 1975.

-----. *Mirar en Bogotá*. Bogota: Biblioteca Básica Colombiana, Instituto Colombiano de Cultura, 1976.

-----. *Mirar en Caracas*. Caracas: Monte Avila Editores, 1974.

-----. *Mothers & Shadows*. Translated by Jo Labanyi. London: Readers International, 1985.

----. *Pasó así*. Montevideo: Arca, 1968.

-----. *Propuesta polémica sobre el arte puertorriqueño*. San Juan: Ediciones Libreria Internacional, 1971

-----. *Seis artistas contemporáneos colombianos*. Bogota: Ediciones Antares, 1963.

-----. *Siglo XX en las artes plásticas latinoamericanas: una gula*. Washington: Endowment for the Arts and Humanities/Museo de Arte Latinamericano de la OEA, 1982-1983.

Uribe, María Tila. *Desde Adento*. Bogota: self-published, 1984.

Valenzuela, Luisa. *Aquí pasan cosas raras*. Buenos Aires: Ediciones de la Flor, 1975.

-----. *Cambio de armas*. Hanover, N.H.: Ediciones del Norte, 1982.

-----. *Clara: Thirteen Stories and a Novel*. Translated by Carpenter, Hortense & Castello. New York: Harcourt Brace Jovanovich, 1976.

-----. *Cola de Lagartija*. Buenos Aires: Bruguera, 1983.

-----. *Como en la guerra*. Buenos Aires: Editorial Sudamericana, 1977.

-----. *Donde viven las águilas*. Buenos Aires: Editorial Celtia, 1983.

-----. *El gato eficaz*. Mexico: Joaquín Mortiz, 1972.

-----. *Hay que sonreir*. Buenos Aires: Editorial Americana, 1966.

-----. *He Who Searches*. Translated by Helen Lane. Elmwood Park, Ill: Dalkey Arch, 1987.

-----. *Libro que no muerde*. Mexico: Universidad Nacional Autónoma de Mexico, 1980.

-----. *Los heréticos*. Buenos Aires: Paidós, 1967.

-----. *Open Door: Stories*. Berkeley, CA: North Point Press, 1988.

-----. *Other Weapons*. Translated by Deborah Bonner. Hanover, N.H.: Ediciones del Norte, 1983.

-----. *Strange Things Happen Here: Twenty-six Short Stories and a Novel*. Translated by Helen Lane. New York: Harcourt Brace Jovanovich, 1979.

-----. *The Lizard's Tale: A Novel*. Translated by Gregory Rabassa. New York: Farrar, Straus & Giroux, 1983.

Vicuña, Cecilia. *Luxumei o el traspié de la doctrina*. Mexico: Editorial Oasis, 1983.

-----. *Precario — Precarious*. Translated by Ann Twitty. New York: Tanman Press, 1983.

Viezzer, Moema. *'Si me permiten hablar...' Testimonio de Domitila, una mujer de las minas de Bolivia*. Mexico: Siglo XXI Editores, 1977.

About the Editor

Alicia Partnoy was born in 1955 in Argentina. As a political activist, she was 'disappeared' and jailed for a total of three years during the recent military dictatorship. She came to the United States as a refugee in 1979. She translates and performs her poetry, which has been set to music by Sweet Honey in the Rock and other groups. Alicia Partnoy lectures extensively at the invitation of Amnesty International, human rights groups and universities, on human rights and writing under repression. She is a translator, and also works at Hispania Books, a Latin American bookstore in Washington, D.C. Alicia Partnoy is the author of *The Little School: Tales of Disappearance and Survival in Argentina* (Cleis Press, 1986), a Writer's Choice selection of the Pushcart Foundation. She lives with her husband and daughter.

CLEIS PRESS

Cleis Press is a nine year old women's publishing company committed to publishing progressive books by women. Order from the office nearest you: *Cleis East,* PO Box 8933, Pittsburgh PA 15221 or *Cleis West,* PO Box 14684, San Francisco CA 94114. Individual orders must be prepaid. Please add 15% shipping/handling. PA and CA residents add sales tax. MasterCard and Visa orders welcome—include account number, exp. date, and signature.

Books from Cleis Press

You Can't Drown the Fire: Latin American Women Writing in Exile edited by Alicia Partnoy. ISBN: 0-939416-16-6 24.95 cloth; ISBN: 0-939416-17-4 9.95 paper.

Unholy Alliances: New Fiction by Women edited by Louise Rafkin. ISBN: 0-939416-14-X 21.95 cloth; ISBN: 0-939416-15-8 9.95 paper.

Sex Work: Writings by Women in the Sex Industry edited by Frédérique Delacoste and Priscilla Alexander. ISBN: 0-939416-10-7 24.95 cloth; ISBN: 0-939416-11-5 9.95 paper.

Different Daughters: A Book by Mothers of Lesbians edited by Louise Rafkin. ISBN: 0-939416-12-3 21.95 cloth; ISBN: 0-939416-13-1 8.95 paper.

The Little School: Tales of Disappearance & Survival in Argentina by Alicia Partnoy. ISBN: 0-939416-08-5 21.95 cloth; ISBN: 0-939416-07-7 8.95 paper.

With the Power of Each Breath: A Disabled Women's Anthology edited by Susan Browne, Debra Connors & Nanci Stern. ISBN: 0-939416-09-3 24.95 cloth; ISBN: 0-939416-06-9 9.95 paper.

Voices in the Night: Women Speaking About Incest edited by Toni A.H. McNaron & Yarrow Morgan. ISBN: 0-939416-02-6 9.95 paper.

Long Way Home: The Odyssey of a Lesbian Mother & Her Children by Jeanne Jullion. ISBN: 0-939416-05-0 8.95 paper.

The Absence of the Dead Is Their Way of Appearing by Mary Winfrey Trautmann. ISBN: 0-939416-04-2 8.95 paper.

Woman-Centered Pregnancy & Birth by the Federation of Feminist Women's Health Centers. ISBN: 0-939416-03-4 11.95 paper.

Fight Back! Feminist Resistance to Male Violence edited by Frédérique Delacoste & Felice Newman. ISBN: 0-939416-01-8 13.95 paper.

On Women Artists: Poems 1975-1980 by Alexandra Grilikhes. ISBN: 0-939416-00-X 4.95 paper.